HAUNTINGS

HAUNTINGS

UNEXPECTED TRUE TALES
OF THE PARANORMAL

PAUL ROLAND

This edition published in 2022 by Arcturus Publishing Limited
26/27 Bickels Yard, 151–153 Bermondsey Street,
London SE1 3HA

AD010615UK

Printed in the UK

CONTENTS

'Where'er we tread 'tis haunted, holy ground'
LORD BYRON (1788–1824)

INTRODUCTION

*'Behind every man now alive stand 30 ghosts, for that is
the ratio by which the dead outnumber the living.'*
ARTHUR C. CLARKE, 2001: *A Space Odyssey*

The dead are all around us. We are surrounded by ghosts, but most
of us are unaware of their presence because we are preoccupied with
our daily routine and our physical needs. In a world of constant and
often violent change we seek stability; we need to be grounded in the
here and now.

I was fortunate in having my first paranormal experiences when I
was very young, so when I began to sense the presence of spirits in
my twenties and later, when I lived in a house that was haunted, I just
accepted it as a fact of life and not as a fearful experience.

The 'haunted' house that I lived in was not the customary
crumbling ruin associated with chain-rattling apparitions but a very

ordinary, modern bungalow and the ghost was not a vengeful spirit but the former owner who, presumably, was simply curious to see his old home again. Neither my wife nor I saw him in the ten years that we lived there, but we sensed his presence on many occasions and it was always in the same location – the former garage which had been his workshop and which we had converted into an office. His presence was so palpable that my wife would frequently look up from her desk expecting to see that I had entered the room. Such incidents suggest that the dead might exist in a state similar to sleep and that their visitations are simply the result of them being drawn back to a location while recalling their former lives. This would account for the fact that most ghosts do not acknowledge the living, but merely drift through the site in a somnambulant state.

THE GHOST WRITER

That ghost was not the only one that has made its presence known to me. I have sensed others on many occasions and almost always when I am writing on an esoteric subject, which suggests that it is the theme, or my frame of mind which attracts them like a lighted match in the darkness. In fact, it is often more than a mere sense that I have. I have felt a gentle caress on my cheek on more than one occasion and the touch of a disembodied hand lightly on the top of my head like that a loving parent or mentor might give to confirm that what I am writing meets his or her approval. Occasionally I have even been quite forcibly prodded in the chest, perhaps playfully or to reprove me for writing something they don't agree with, but I find it reassuring. I have no fear of phantoms as I am a firm believer in the old saying, 'like attracts like', and my own considerable experience as a teacher of psychic development and meditation has appeared to confirm that.

Of course, my invisible visitors might not be ghosts at all, but guides or guardian angels, but I don't think that the name we give disembodied entities is of importance. Sensing their presence is sufficient to signify that there is another reality beyond our physical world, a belief that appears to be confirmed by the countless number of near-death experiences reported by people of diverse beliefs and backgrounds around the world from ancient times to the present day. I have personally experienced the out-of-body state several times since childhood and found it a liberating and exhilarating experience. In fact, it stimulated my interest in investigating all forms of paranormal phenomena. So for me at least, ghosts are not something to be feared, but a fascinating anomaly.

Other people have been less fortunate, as the stories in the following pages will show, but it is my understanding that spirits are essentially the same personalities that they were during their lives. So I would attribute all unpleasant or disturbing experiences to encounters with malevolent personalities who resent sharing their possessions or personal space with the living. There is, however, another and more dangerous category of ghost and that is the addictive or psychotic personality who seeks to indulge its addiction vicariously by latching like a parasite on to a like-minded individual with whom it has an affinity. Any type of addiction will attract these individuals; drugs, alcohol, violence, excessive greed, unnatural lust and even an obsession with dangerous pursuits. But I believe all of these malevolent spirits are human. Despite anecdotal 'evidence' to the contrary I cannot accept the existence of 'evil' spirits or demons. The section on modern exorcists that I have included is by way of acknowledging how willingly we project our fears on to mythical and imaginary entities in a desperate attempt to explain what we cannot comprehend. By giving these imaginary entities power over us we are stifling our development and understanding of the greater reality of which we are a part. Ignorance, in this case, is not bliss but a backward step into the mists and superstitions of the Dark Ages. Just as the more open-minded scientists and some of the more serious parapsychologists have shown, many incidents of poltergeist activity are kinetic disturbances generated unconsciously by adolescents experiencing the conflicting emotions of puberty, so similarly many of the supposed victims of demonic possession can be diagnosed as

When things go flying for no apparent reason, it could be the work of a poltergeist.

being psychologically disturbed. Attributing their disorders to the work of demons and subjecting these impressionable individuals to what must amount to physical abuse is reprehensible to say the least. However, after reading the evidence, you may disagree.

My personal experiences have provided ample evidence of the existence of the soul and its survival after death, but that does not mean that I, nor anyone sharing my convictions, can afford to make definitive statements regarding any form of phenomenon. Each experience only reveals one piece of the puzzle, one fleeting glimpse into a greater reality which we cannot grasp with the limited processing power of the human brain. We must also be acutely aware that as human beings we all share the unfortunate tendency to jump to conclusions when we think that doing so will confirm our personal beliefs and prejudices. In this respect, I am as guilty as anyone and offer the following story as an example of how easily we can deceive ourselves.

THE GHOST WHO WASN'T THERE

Recently my family and I moved into a new home. Shortly afterwards we were awoken one morning at 3am by what sounded like a bookcase or some other piece of heavy furniture being overturned. I crawled bleary-eyed out of bed and systematically searched the house from top to bottom but found nothing untoward. The next night it happened again. And again the next. Each time it startled me out of my sleep. Convinced that it had to be a ghost, I was seriously considering performing some kind of 'clearing' rite when I discovered the source of the disturbance.

On the fourth morning I happened to wake up shortly before 3am and went to the second-floor bathroom which overlooks the street. As I stood by the window I heard footsteps approaching and then that unmistakable clattering sound which in my sleep had sounded even louder. It was the sound of a thick bundle of newspapers being dropped through the letterbox! Such an explanation would never have occurred to me. Who could imagine that some old man with insomnia would take it upon himself to deliver newspapers at 3am and that the noise would be amplified in a silent house to such an extent that it could be mistaken for falling furniture?

As I said, we are all prey to making assumptions, especially if they confirm our beliefs or justify our prejudices.

A scientist who values their name and reputation will be wary of stating any facts regarding a phenomenon for fear that they may be proven wrong when more facts come to light and this, I believe, should be applied with equal vigour to the paranormal as we cannot measure or quantify any aspect of a world we cannot see, but only sense. The only thing we can state with certainty, to paraphrase Shakespeare, is that there are more things in heaven and earth than we might care to know about. Whether these are friendly or not, you can decide for yourself after reading this book.

'It is wonderful that five thousand years have now elapsed since the creation of the world, and still it is undecided whether or not there has ever been an instance of the spirit of any person appearing after death. All argument is against it; but all belief is for it.'
SAMUEL JOHNSON, *The Life of Samuel Johnson*

CHAPTER ONE

WHAT IS A GHOST?

Ghosts are not a supernatural phenomenon but a purely natural one. It is generally accepted that they are either earthbound spirits or residual personal energy which lingers at a location which was significant to the individual in life or at the moment of their death.

Our fear comes from our vain attempts to deny the existence of these apparitions and not from any power that they can hold over the living.

'If we could take a material man and dissolve away his physical constituent without interfering with the sense-data by means of which we perceive him, we should be left with, exactly, an apparition.'

G.N.M. Tyrrell, *Apparitions*, 1953

Colorado-based parapsychologist Jeff Danelek has become something of a ghost-hunters' guru after presenting a compelling argument for the existence of spirits in his influential study *The Case For Ghosts* (Llewellyn, 2006). In place of the usual sensationalistic stories of playful poltergeists and other paranormal phenomena, Jeff approaches the subject in an objective, down-to-earth manner that has earned him the respect of both the scientific community and other paranormal investigators.

WORKING THINGS OUT

During the course of writing this book I asked him to share his theories with me and explain how he reached his thought-provoking conclusions.

'I noticed that most of the stories I came across – especially those that dealt with interactive communications between spirits and humans – almost invariably centred around similar themes – namely, a certain over-attachment to a place or person, or a fear or uncertainty about moving on. Very few ghosts, it seems, appeared particularly happy or indifferent to their plight, forcing me to wonder if it wasn't certain mindsets that were keeping them effectively bound to our world when, by all reason, they should be moving on to the joy of the ethereal realm. Noticing that living human beings also tended to keep themselves stuck in undesirable circumstances (stress, jealousy, materialism, addiction, depression) often as a result of an unwillingness to acknowledge – much less attempt to change – their attitudes, I simply wondered what would happen to such people when they died. As such, my understanding of ghostly psychology is largely based upon what I understand about human psychology in general; I simply took it to the next level and tried to visualize how materialism, stubbornness and anger (among other attitudes) might

Jeff Danalek.

impact on the disembodied energy of a deceased person. It really wasn't that difficult to do, especially considering that a ghost (which I define exclusively to be the disembodied conscious energy of a once living human being) is every bit as human when dead as they were alive and, therefore, just as prone to making the same bad decisions and maintaining the same counterproductive attitudes as they did in life. This, in fact, is why I believe they are ghosts in the first place and why being an earthbound spirit is such a predicament.'

Jeff has identified various categories of ghost which he believes equate with recognizable personality types.

CATEGORIES OF GHOST

'The first thing to understand about a ghost is that where human beings are concerned, not even death can change things. I believe that when a person dies, they move on to the next realm with all the personality traits, quirks, prejudices, biases, and a lifetime of accumulated wisdom – and nonsense – fully intact. Working from that premise, then, it's not difficult to imagine how some people would either choose to become a ghost or might find themselves trapped on the physical plane by their own personality flaws. As such, we might assume that the reasons for becoming a ghost may be as numerous and varied as are the types of personalities humans exhibit.'

THE UNAWARE GHOST

'Many paranormal investigators believe that some entities may remain within the physical realm simply because they are not aware that they are dead. As such, they go on about their life much as they did before, completely oblivious to the fact that they are no longer a part of the physical realm and remain that way until some sudden trauma or realization goads them into either remembering that they have died or

demonstrates that they are, in fact, no longer among the living. This idea has been popularized by such excellent movies as The Sixth Sense *and* The Others *and is a part of many people's beliefs about ghosts (a perception Hollywood has done much to reinforce).*

'I, however, find it extremely unlikely that ghosts don't know they're dead. Near-death experience (NDE) accounts remain remarkably consistent in their insistence that even upon sudden and unexpected death the soul invariably detaches from the body and hovers about nearby, all the while aware of its surroundings and cognizant of the fact that it is no longer attached to its physical body. If these accounts are accurate portrayals of what the human psyche experiences at the moment of death, it seems that to not be aware of the fact that one had 'passed over' would be about as hard to miss as would be the loss of a limb; some things, it seems, are just a little too obvious not to notice. Unless they died in their sleep or were so inebriated when they passed that they never knew what hit them, I should imagine the one thing they could not help but notice is their own death, especially once one started encountering deceased loved ones and, perhaps, various religious figures. As such, I seriously doubt that any recently deceased spirit would be in – or, at least, remain in – a state of ignorance for long. It simply doesn't hold together logically.'

Jeff has an original explanation to explain the disproportionate number of earthbound spirits of children that have been reported.

'It is possible that children or the mentally incapacitated might not recognize the situation for what it is and remain attached to the physical plane after their death. Ghosts of children are frequent subjects of a haunting, leading to the possibility that children who are unable to comprehend death in practical terms may well be too confused to move on after their demise. Death is, after all, generally considered a "grown-up"

affair that is rarely discussed with children. As such, some may have no real understanding of what is happening to them and so remain trapped in a type of "sleep state" until they either can finally comprehend what has happened and move on or are rescued by other spiritual entities whose job it is to look out for these gentle souls and guide them along.'

THE DENIAL GHOST

'Just as there are people who make denial a major part of their life, it is only natural to imagine that there are those personalities who will make it an integral part of their afterlife as well and so will simply refuse to accept the truth of their own earthly demise. They can be the ones who remain earthbound the longest, for human pride can be as powerful and debilitating on the other side as it often proves to be on this side of eternity, which can make it especially difficult to convince them to give up the charade and move on.'

THE ATTACHED GHOST

'This type of ghost is so emotionally attached to the things of the world that it refuses to let go of them. This is often their home or some place they truly loved. And so they stay behind, always hovering on the edge of human perception, but rarely if ever able to interact with it in any meaningful way.

'Such ghosts often remain around for years, or even decades, so great is their attachment to the things of the world. They tend to be the more possessive ghosts who insist that new residents leave their home, or attempt to interfere in the lives of those they left behind. Over-identification with one's profession or trade can also produce this effect – ghosts of librarians or school janitors, for instance, are examples of this – and elderly couples and shut-ins who have learned to isolate themselves from the outside world especially run this risk.'

THE JEALOUS GHOST

'Though exceedingly rare, there are accounts of ghostly entities attaching themselves not to things, but to people, and interjecting themselves into earthly relationships, usually out of some misguided notion of possessiveness or outright jealousy. This could be anything from an over-possessive spouse that can't accept the thought of their mate remarrying, to a spurned lover who took his or her own life only to come back and attach themselves to the source of their unrequited affections later. Active only around the source of their possessiveness and then usually only when in the presence of that source's newfound affections, the jealous ghost can be among the most tenacious and frightening ghosts of all.'

THE FEARFUL GHOST

'Due to cultural or religious conditioning, some personalities are simply too afraid to find out what fate has in store for them and so prefer the mundane existence of a haunting to the potential punishment a final judgement might portend. Often these are individuals who did considerable harm – or believe they did – to others and so fear being held to account for their offences and punished. To them, then, remaining within the comparative safety of the physical realm is their only means of avoiding this judgement and the punishment they believe they so richly deserve, and so they cling to the material world the way a frightened child might cling to its mother's leg on the first day of school.

'It's not just evil-doers who find themselves in this state, however; ordinary people who have had strong religious beliefs drilled into them from childhood and feel they have not lived up to them are good candidates to become fearful ghosts, especially if they believe God is angry with them and they have not had a chance to "repent" or had their sins absolved by a priest before they died. Fear is almost as strong an emotion as love, and can keep one tied to the earth plane as completely as denial, possessiveness *and jealousy can, and is easily capable of making us our own worst enemy and more adroit at inadvertently torturing ourselves than any external foe – or Deity – could ever be.'*

THE MELANCHOLY OR SAD GHOST

'Perhaps the most depressing type of entity one can encounter, the "sad" ghost is someone who is so overwhelmed by some tragedy that they continue to wander the physical realm as if in a state of shock that they seem unable to recover from.

'Suicides often end up as "sad" ghosts, for the same factors that drove them to take their own lives frequently keep them bound to the very physical realm they took such pains to rid themselves of. As such, they can also be among the most difficult to "rescue", for they are often too self-absorbed in their own pain to either recognize the need for salvation or care about it. They truly are the most lost of all souls and may require significant intervention on both the part of the living and other spiritual entities to pull them towards the light.'

THE MISSION GHOST

'This type of ghost stays around in order to take care of some unfinished business that was cut short by their unexpected death. This "mission" can be as simple as revealing the location of a hidden will, or as major as trying to find justice for a life cut short by murder, but in either case mission ghosts seem intent upon achieving some goal they've set before themselves and feel they cannot rest until they have succeeded.'

THE GOODBYE OR COMFORT GHOST

'The goodbye ghost is a manifestation that appears – often only once – to either say goodbye to a loved one bereaved by their loss or to simply assure them that they are well and have passed over successfully. These can

manifest as electrical phenomena or something as dramatic as a full-body manifestation. Tales of widows seeing their late husbands sitting on the foot of their bed or children encountering the manifestation of their dead sibling in their bedroom are legion, and even recently departed family pets have been occasionally reported. Trauma and excessive grief may account for some cases, but certainly not for all of them.'

THE CURIOUS GHOST

'I'd imagine that those personalities who in life demonstrated a curiosity about the afterlife or were of a scientific bent might find the chance to manipulate matter and energy from the other side to be too good an opportunity to pass up. I'd suspect such personalities, however, to be fairly rare and frequently frustrated in their efforts to get through to us "thick mortals", and so wonder if they might not be prone to tiring of the game and move on to explore other realms of the spirit.'

THE MISCHIEVOUS GHOST

'Similar to the curious ghost but of a somewhat more menacing vein is that which we call the mischievous or "playful" ghost.

'It is different from the curious ghost in that it isn't as interested in demonstrating the reality of the supernatural realm as it is in simply frightening the still living. It is as though haunting is one great amusement to it, and it will spend any amount of energy necessary to play the game for as long as it can. Such ghosts are immature and childish (like the personalities behind them) and are comparable to the practical joker who thinks everything he does is hilarious and can't understand why others can't see the humour.

'This can manifest itself in something as innocent as moving furniture, hiding a piece of jewellery or pulling the sheets off a bed, to physical assault! They want to make a nuisance of themselves and, in fact, go out of their way to make living with them almost impossible.

'They may be the source of at least some poltergeist activity. A nervous teenage girl may simply be the perfect conduit for a mischievous entity to manifest or do its mischief.'

THE ANGRY GHOST

'People have been willing to endure tremendous hardship and great personal loss in the quest for revenge, so the thought that an angry personality might be willing to endure the personal hell of an earthly wandering in search of vengeance is not difficult to imagine.

'Fortunately such entities are relatively rare, but even so they present the greatest challenge to the ghost-hunter. Anger is a destructive force that grows more powerful with time and can only be dissipated through the power of love and compassion.'

CHAPTER TWO

CITY OF THE DEAD

Every city in the world has its share of ghosts, but surely none is more deserving of its reputation as the capital of the uncanny than Edinburgh. With its narrow, twisting alleyways, cobbled streets and ancient, imposing buildings the Old Town resembles the set of a Hammer horror movie. All it needs is a shroud of creeping fog and one can imagine its more unsavoury inhabitants stalking the streets again.

Other cities have their serial killers and criminals, but Edinburgh can boast a whole rogues gallery, enough to fill the chamber of horrors in Madame Tussauds several times over.

Long before Hannibal Lecter put cannibalistic killers on the menu, Edinburgh was home to real-life people-eater Sawney Bean. Then there were the bodysnatchers Burke and Hare, cross-eyed lady-killer Dr Neil Cream and criminal mastermind Deacon Brodie, the inspiration for Robert Louis Stevenson's *Dr Jekyll and Mr Hyde*. In fact several of Edinburgh's larger-than-life personalities served as the models for immortal literary figures, including Sherlock Holmes and his nemesis Professor Moriarty. Conan Doyle studied medicine at Edinburgh University and based the master detective on his own teacher and mentor Dr Joseph Bell. Charles Dickens made only a brief sojourn to the city, but he returned with the seed for what is arguably the most famous ghost story ever written, *A Christmas Carol*. And let's not forget that his spiritual descendant, J.K. Rowling, conjured up her finest creation, the boy wizard Harry Potter, in a café overlooking Greyfriars Graveyard.

But if it's 'real' history you're wanting, then your first stop must be the oldest haunted site in Edinburgh, which lies just outside the city. As everyone who has read *The Da Vinci Code*, or seen the movie based on Dan Brown's best-seller, will know, the 15th-century chapel at Roslin is the centre of an alleged conspiracy concerning the true fate of Jesus of Nazareth and his supposed descendants, proof of which is said to be hidden in sealed vaults underneath the chapel. The hype surrounding the book has attracted thousands of tourists from around the world who might not have been so keen to linger had they known that the chapel is haunted by an order of Augustine monks known as the Black Canons. Judith Fiskin, a former archivist and curator at Roslin, claims to have seen a ghostly monk during her tenure in the 1980s and to have shared the experience with several reliable witnesses. But the brothers are not the only spirits wandering around. The site is also said to be haunted by the restless spirit of a mason's apprentice, reputedly killed by his master for having outshone his mentor by carving what is known as the Apprentice Pillar.

Animal spirits are also to be seen when conditions are favourable. According to local legend the spirit of a murdered hound can be seen and heard prowling the grounds of nearby Roslin Castle. The Mauthe Dog, as it is known, was cruelly put to death beside its English master during the Battle of Roslin in 1303 at which the Scots routed an English army of more than 30,000. Bad losers, the Sassenachs.

There is even a local 'white lady' identified as Lady Bothwell, who was evicted from her ancestral home by the heartless Regent Moray in the late 16th century. Presumably, she returns to search in vain for her tormentor and tear his merciless heart from his body.

ARTHUR'S SEAT

Wife-murderer Nicol Muschat was hanged here in 1720. It is also the site of the burial place of the city's plague victims. Nearby Salisbury Crags was at one time the preferred jumping spot for suicides. Many others met their deaths at this precarious peak by accident and no doubt, foul play played its part in the premature demise of many more.

In 1836, some children made a curious find while playing at Arthur's Seat – 17 miniature coffins, each with a doll inside. Could it have been a memorial to unknown murder victims? Or part of a satanic ritual?

BARONY STREET

A local coven known as the 'Witches Howff' were burned alive in a house in this street in the 17th century, just 13 of an estimated 300 women burned for practising the 'old religion' in Edinburgh at the time.

PICARDY PLACE, TOP OF LEITH WALK

The birthplace of Sir Arthur Conan Doyle and formerly the site of public executions.

NO. 5 HAZELDEAN TERRACE

In 1957 Edinburgh was able to boast two active poltergeists, both of which attracted national headlines. By all accounts the Rothesay Place poltergeist put on a fair show of strength, but came a poor second to the Hazeldean mischief-maker, which frequently threw a wooden chopping board and other kitchen utensils and crockery at the startled inhabitants. Being made of stronger stuff than their Sassenach cousins down south, the residents of Hazeldean Terrace braved out the assault and eventually the activity died down.

EDINBURGH PLAYHOUSE, GREENSIDE PLACE

Like all old theatres, the Playhouse claims to have a disembodied employee doing the rounds after dark, in this case an elderly man in a grey coat whom the staff refer to affectionately as 'Albert'. He is believed to have been either a stagehand who perished in an accident or a nightwatchman who topped himself.

Alternatively, he may have been just another victim of Edinburgh's rough justice as Greenside Place was once the site of the public scaffold.

ROYAL LYCEUM THEATRE, LOTHIAN ROAD

The actress Ellen Terry is said to haunt the stage on which she made her theatrical debut in 1856.

GILLESPIE CRESCENT, BRUNTSFIELD

On this site once stood a celebrated haunted house known as The Wrychtishousis. In the 18th century it was the scene for regular visits by a headless woman who was believed to be the wife of James Clerk, who died leaving her and her baby to the tender mercies of his homicidal brother. With James out of the way the brother murdered her in order to inherit the house, but he brought too short a trunk and had to cut her head off to get her body inside it. Then he hid the box in the cellar. Just another gruesome old legend? Nope. Her headless corpse and that of her child were unearthed by workmen when the house was being demolished, together with the killer's written confession.

BALCARRES STREET, MORNINGSIDE

The Green Lady of Balcarres Street is said to be the restless spirit of Elizabeth Pittendale, wife of the 18th-century landowner Sir Thomas Elphinstone. He reputedly caught her in a compromising position with his son by a former marriage and stabbed her to death before committing suicide, leaving his son to inherit his estate.

GILMERTON GRANGE

A similar melodrama occurred in the 14th century where this farmhouse bearing the same name now stands. Landowner Sir John Herring had forbidden his daughter Margaret from meeting her lover on this spot, but she defied him. In a fit of pique Sir John set the building ablaze with his daughter inside. Evidently, she still hasn't forgiven him, for her spirit has walked that spot for around seven hundred years.

EDINBURGH FESTIVAL THEATRE, NICOLSON STREET

This is the former site of the Empire Palace Theatre, where illusionist Sigmund Neuberger (aka 'the Great Lafayette') was burned to death in 1911 after a fire broke out during his act. Nine stagehands and Neuberger's stage double also perished in the blaze.

THE CORN EXCHANGE, BALTIC STREET

More grisly goings-on here, the site of several child murders in the 19th century. The killer was a former publican who hanged himself before his neighbours could lynch him. It is said that his victims can be heard crying in the night. Producers of the American TV series *Understanding the Paranormal* claimed to have caught the culprit on film.

THE DOVECOT, DOVECOT ROAD, CORSTORPHINE

The White Lady of Corstorphine haunts this spot and can be seen brandishing a sword, the very same one with which she skewered her drunken lover. She was beheaded in 1679 after an unsuccessful escape attempt.

CRAIGCROOK CASTLE, CORSTORPHINE HILL

All castles boast a resident ghost and Craigcrook is no exception. Its most famous owner, the author and Lord Advocate Lord Francis Jeffrey, drew his last breath here in 1850. His presence is said to be the cause of cold spots, phantom footsteps and a doorbell that rings of its own accord.

CAROLINE PARK HOUSE (AKA ROYSTON HOUSE), GRANTON

The deceased wife of a former owner, Sir James Mackenzie has been seen to glide soundlessly through a wall at midnight and pass into the main entrance before reappearing in the east courtyard to the incessant ringing of an old bell. Locals know her as 'The Green Lady'.

BORTHWICK CASTLE, GOREBRIDGE

Now a hotel, its Red Room is haunted by a young girl thought to be the spiteful spirit of Anne Grant, a peasant's daughter, said to be responsible for slamming doors on gentlemen's fingers. Local legend has it that she had been deflowered by her employer, Lord Borthwick, who murdered her to ensure his secret was safe. Exorcisms have failed to dislodge her.

CRICHTON CASTLE, MIDLOTHIAN

This imposing fortification is haunted by a figure on horseback who rides through the castle wall. It is thought to be Sir William Crichton, Chancellor of Scotland in the 15th century. It was he who organized the 'Black Dinner' in 1440 at Edinburgh Castle, to which the Earl of Douglas and his brother, both of whom were children, were invited. This was to dine with the boy king James II. Since they were contenders to the throne they were murdered when they arrived.

DALHOUSIE CASTLE, LASSWADE

The 'Grey Lady' walks the clammy corridors of this formidable fortress. She is believed to be the mistress of one of the lairds, whose jealous wife contrived to lure her to the castle where she was imprisoned and starved to death.

MOUNT LOTHIAN QUARRY, PENICUIK

Edinburgh has its own phantom horseman, but this one is no mere urban legend. It has its origins in historical fact. In the late 19th century a young labourer took his master's horse without permission to pay a call on his lover. At the quarry, he came upon a man pinned under his overturned cart, but instead of riding for help he rode on, presumably because he was desperate to avoid discovery. The injured man subsequently died, but not before he was able to tell his friends of the incident and describe the man who failed to help him. Vowing revenge, the friends are said to have tracked down and hung the young man who now rides past the spot driven, so to speak, by a guilty conscience.

THE UNDERGROUND CITY

The focus of many of the city's supernatural encounters is the area around Edinburgh Castle known as the underground city. It's not actually a city, more of a labyrinth of tunnels and cavernous chambers carved out of the crag and tail on which the castle and Royal Mile were built. The ground beneath this long sloping street is composed of soft sandstone and the top of it towered so high above the rest of the city that it could be excavated from the side. When overcrowding in the city was at its height in the early years of the 18th century, the poor carved out their own living quarters from the rock to shelter from the worst of the Scottish weather and the authorities let them be as it eased pressure on the workhouses. Needless to say, many perished in the intolerable conditions from hunger, cold, disease and periodic cave-ins. Their spirits are thought to account for the moaning and wailing heard by the shopkeepers brave enough to venture down into their basement stock rooms after dark.

The world beneath the streets was expanded considerably at the end of the 18th century when the influx of migrant Irish workers put the city under greater strain. But Scottish engineers came up with an ingenious solution. They constructed a network of bridges to connect the central ridge to the surrounding hills and then built houses and shops around them to obscure the structures. The vaults under these viaducts were intended as cellars and storehouses for local traders, but when it was discovered that they were not waterproof the merchants moved out and the migrants moved in. Their existence was almost forgotten until social reformers evicted them some years

The moaning and wailing that is heard is thought to emanate from those who perished many years ago.

later and crowded them into the tenements which became ghettos for the underprivileged.

In 1845 reformer Dr George Bell, M.D. visited Blackfriars Wynd, next to the South Bridge in an effort to publicize the living conditions of the beggars and hawkers who lived there.

'In a vault or cave under a large tenement, reside an old man, his invalid wife, and his two daughters, one of whom has a natural child and the other of whom is paralytic. The man has an air of respectability about him, but the family has no visible means of living. There were three beds in the vault; and on investigating the matter, (we) found that the said vault is a lodging house, and is often tenanted to repletion. This man is the type of class who live by subletting their miserable and dark abodes to as many as can be crammed into them. In another vault in the wynd we found a very fat Irishwoman, a widow, a pauper, and the mother of six children. By her own confession she occasionally takes in a lodger – in reality, however, she accommodates two or three all the year round.'

It is here in creepy places such as Mary King's Close, the South Bridge Vaults and the Black Mausoleum in Greyfriars Graveyard that the most recent and disturbing sightings have taken place.

HAUNTED HOT SPOTS

Arguably the most notorious haunted spot in the city is Mary King's Close, named after the daughter of a prosperous local merchant. The legends associated with this location are lurid and legion and centre on the victims of the plague of 1645 who were imprisoned by the city elders. Their jailers then locked the gates at both ends of the close for fear that the contagion might spread. This rather draconian measure saved the city from the scourge of the sickness, but none

Mary King's Close: Shadowy residents include 'The Worried Man' and a lady who appears at the end of the close and then vanishes.

of the residents of Mary King's Close survived. Their decomposing corpses were later hacked up and the remains buried in an area known as The Meadows. No one would live in the close after that, or even go near it after dark for fear that the spirits of the dead would reach through the gates and drag them inside.

Its reputation as a haunting 'hot spot' remains undimmed to this day. As recently as 1992 a documentary film crew arrived with a Japanese psychic named Aiko Gibo. On entering one of the houses she claimed to be able to see an apparition in one corner of a room where several psychics had mentioned sensing a cold spot some months before. Gibo described this 'spirit' as a 10-year-old girl wearing a dirty white dress and boots. When asked for its name, Gibo was given the answer 'Annie'. Gibo and Annie communicated telepathically as Annie asked why her mother had abandoned her and where her favourite doll could be. When Gibo returned with a new doll Annie seemed comforted and more communicative. All of this could be put down to the imagination of the medium were it not for the fact that a short while later a female visitor to the site who had known nothing of the broadcast screamed when she entered the room, claiming to have seen a little girl in the corner whose face was disfigured by sores. Research has unearthed the fact that a woman by the name of Jean Mackenzie and her little girl were forcibly quarantined in the house during the plague. It was not established whether the little girl's name was Annie, but it seems likely as it was a common name at that time. After the documentary was broadcast the number of visitors to the site increased dramatically, many of them leaving dolls for the little ghost to play with.

Other shadowy residents of the close include 'The Worried Man', who walks back and forth as if brooding on some dark deed he is planning, or perhaps he is simply searching for something. At other times a woman in black appears for a moment at the end of the close and then just as mysteriously vanishes, as does a young boy at the same location. A male figure, presumably a storekeeper, has been seen suspended in mid-air beneath the 'plague room' window at the spot where a staircase had once been and a middle-aged woman has been known to put in an appearance at the top of the steps leading into the street. If anyone is brave enough to venture inside the derelict houses they are sure to hear sufficient scratching, whispering and boisterous phantom carousing to convince them that some of the former residents are extremely reluctant to leave, despite its grim reputation.

THE HAUNTED VAULT

Among the many tales told of uncanny encounters in the South Bridge Vaults, the case of Marion Duffy and her six-year-old daughter Claire must rank as one of the most chilling.

Marion had serious doubts about joining a guided tour with such a young child in tow, but Claire had reassured her mother that she wouldn't be afraid. Even when the party entered the claustrophobic chamber deep underground the little girl lost none of her eagerness to explore. She joined in the nervous giggles and squeezed her mother's hand reassuringly as she might have done if they were going on a fairground ghost train. It was only when the guide turned off her torch to heighten the spooky atmosphere that Marion regretted letting her daughter talk her into taking the tour.

'Don't worry Claire,' she said. 'It's all just for show.' A small hand responded with a gentle squeeze. Then the grip became tighter. Evidently Claire was afraid. Very afraid. The grip tightened still further until Marion realized that she couldn't pull herself free. It was becoming painful. Instinctively she pulled hard and kicked, not caring in that moment if Claire was hurt as the pain was unbearable. But it couldn't be Claire. No child would be capable of such a vice-like grip. She kicked harder and in doing so lost her balance. She collided with the person standing next to her in the dark who screamed that something was attacking her and the next instant there was a mad scramble for the exit.

When the guide switched the torch back on Marion found herself surrounded by strangers, all with a look of embarrassment on their faces. Claire was nowhere to be seen. Then her mother spotted her on the other side of the vault. Shaking with a mixture of fear and relief the little girl explained that when the light went out a hand had gripped hers and led her to the far end of the vault. She knew it wasn't her mother's hand, but she had been too frightened to cry out. Asked how she knew it wasn't her mother's hand, she replied, 'Because it had claws.'

GREYFRIARS GRAVEYARD

> *'Greyfriars is the most haunted spot in the*
> *country's most haunted city.'*
>
> The Weekly News

Greyfriars is known locally as a 'thin place', a site where the veil between this world and the next is believed to be so fragile that spirits can pass through it. Its reputation presumably grew from the fact that it was the site of mass graves following the great plague of 1568 when countless thousands of diseased corpses were flung into a huge pit and from the fact that it was the custom to display the heads of executed criminals on its gate posts. A grisly lot, the Scots.

Twelve hundred survivors of the Covenanter movement (Scots

Presbyterians) were imprisoned in the Covenanters' Prison on the orders of Charles II after their defeat at the Battle of Bothwell Brig and many of them starved to death or died from disease. Of the remainder, many thousands were executed by the King's Advocate, 'Bloody' George Mackenzie. Mackenzie was buried in Greyfriars in 1691 within sight of the Covenanters' Prison and the graves of those he had condemned to death. Not surprisingly perhaps, this inspired a host of macabre ghost stories including one in which 'Bloody' Mackenzie's coffin is said to move within the tomb, known as the Black Mausoleum, because he is restless and tormented in death.

'I experienced a feeling like something placing its hands on my chest and pushing me gently backwards inside the Covenanters Prison.'

Mackenzie had company for Christmas in 1879 when the city council disinterred hundreds of rotting corpses from St Giles' cemetery and unceremoniously dumped them in nearby Greyfriars. Visitors who climb the hill to look down on the town are unaware that they are actually standing on a mountain of dead bodies.

SPIRITS PUT TO THE TEST

'. . . hauntings do not just happen. It is not merely by chance that you are there when the ghost walks. A physical presence is needed not only to see the apparition but perhaps to cause it to appear.'

ANTONY D. HIPPISLEY COXE, *Haunted Britain*, 1973

With so many spirit sightings it was inevitable that sooner or later the parapsychologists would investigate Edinburgh's hottest spots.

The most serious study was conducted in the vaults off South Niddry Street by a team headed by Dr Richard Wiseman, who measured the magnetic fields, light levels, air temperature and movement. Members of the public were invited to visit the vaults while the experiment was in progress and to write down their experiences.

The usual 'disturbances' were duly reported. These perhaps predictably included strange odours and the sense of being watched, but Dr Wiseman's team attributed these to imperceptible changes in the atmospheric conditions.

'These alleged hauntings do not represent evidence for "ghostly" activity, but are instead the result of people responding – perhaps unwittingly – to "normal" factors in their surroundings.'

British Journal of Psychology, 2003

Such mundane explanations do not, however, explain many visitors' often violent reactions to the atmosphere in the 'haunted vault' off Niddry Street or indeed to the Black Mausoleum which is situated in Greyfriars Graveyard, neither of which were investigated by the scientists, something which is beginning to look more and more like an oversight.

Nor do these environmental changes take any account at all of the physical marks, scratches, bruising and torn-out hair which have been reported to the tour operators by so many visitors. The following accounts are just a small sample of those received.

EYEWITNESS ACCOUNTS

'We had not been in the Black Mausoleum long when we started hearing knocking noises coming from beneath us, which steadily grew louder and seemed to move up and round the walls. I was standing at the back and I felt the temperature drop, even though it was a very warm night. I started physically shaking, even though I was wearing several jumpers, and had pins and needles in my feet and arms. I then felt myself go freezing cold and the next thing I remember is waking up lying on the ground. My friend had also collapsed. The next morning, I woke up to find that I had three deep scratches on my stomach – there is no way this could have been caused by my falling, as I was wearing several layers. My friend Lewis also had scratches on his arm.

'I decided to go back again, this time with a group of different friends. I experienced the same sensations – the feeling of cold, pins and needles, and shaking, followed by the inevitable black-out and scratches on my arms the next morning.'

Camilla Davidson

'On my first tour I was part of the "mass poltergeist attack" where the whole tour heard knocking and both myself and another girl fainted. The second time I heard knocking again and again I fainted. I felt something kneel beside me, actually touching my leg. I was terrified and was crying, but felt I was unable to open my eyes.'

Debbie Stephen

'As you might know there were a number of attacks/strange happenings on the 10 o'clock tour last Saturday. Two men and a woman collapsed and remained unconscious for a minute or so, while people inside heard weird noises. Being a huge sceptic I find it hard to believe these people

The Black Mausoleum (on the right), which hides its dark character during daylight.

could have been actors. If they were, then they were damn good. To be honest, while standing inside in the back, I felt something like cold spots on my legs. That's when I left . . .'

Jeroen Remmerswaal

'I thought you might like to add this experience to your archive, as I was so spooked I'm afraid I fled without really speaking to any of your colleagues. I'd been on the tour the previous August and experienced a feeling like something placing its hands on my chest and pushing me gently backwards inside the Covenanters' Prison, and then I'd been in the centre of a cold spot inside the mausoleum. Again when we went inside the prison, I felt the sensation of being pushed backwards.

'Without warning something tugged on the end of my watch strap, hard. I was wearing a jacket that covered my watch, and my arm was wrapped around my friend. If it was someone trying to mess about, for them to have found their way inside the cuff of my jacket and then found the end of my watch strap, without either myself or my friend feeling something, would have been impossible.

'After this, we went to the bar, where the spookiest thing of all happened. Over a hefty dose of whisky, we watched scratches that tingled like nettle rash come up on the first two knuckles of both of my hands – my friend had hold of my hand and would have known if anything had scratched me or I had scratched myself.

'No offence, but I'm not going on that tour again. Twice was enough, I think a third time might be chancing my luck!'

Alix Cavanagh

'I felt as if the temperature was gradually falling – nothing unusual there, it being the middle of January. However, another member of the tour ran out stating she simply "needed to leave".

'*Once she had gone someone began pulling at my hair. There was no one behind me and I knew those around me couldn't be doing it – they were too far forward. It was a repeated insistent tugging. A few days afterwards the back of my head felt incredibly cold and the hair began falling out from a very concentrated area – the area I felt that had been pulled at.*'

Louise Wright

'*I hit a cold patch that chilled me to my very bones. A woman grabbed my left arm and then the cold hit us both really hard as if the wind had become a "being" or a "wall". She panicked and ran from the place. I noticed that I was swaying and when I looked around at the silhouettes, everyone was swaying . . . The lady behind me was swaying so much she grabbed me to stop herself from passing out.*'

Jenny Bosson

'*Standing at the back of the Black Mausoleum I kept feeling someone, or should it be something, breathing in my face. This was a little unnerving as everyone was facing the front of the mausoleum!*'

Christine Hornsby

'*I felt frozen solid all over the whole time, i.e. I couldn't move and I don't think it was just fear because I tried to move my hand and I couldn't. All I can remember doing is praying to God that nothing would touch me, and that I've never felt so scared in my entire life.*'

Josh Blinco

'*I felt a sensation of extreme cold, dizziness and nausea. I put this sensation down to nerves. It was only when I returned to my hotel that*

I noticed a series of deep and increasingly painful scratches on my back, abdomen and chest.'

Kenny J Gray

'I distinctly felt a man's hand grab my arm twice. Something brushed past me and hit me on the elbow and it punched my sister on the back. Later she was complaining of a sore back and we discovered scratch marks.'

Debbie Reid

'Suddenly my husband moved away from me. As I tried to pull him back he stiffened and then began to wobble. He shakily told me something had "run up and down his back". When we finally left the tomb he was visibly shaken.'

Helen Davidson

'After being in the tomb for a couple of minutes I started to hear heavy scratching noises at the back. I saw a girl looking up at the exact same time to the exact same spot as if listening to the scratching as well. Back on the Royal Mile I saw the girl again, and she described the exact same location (at the back and top of the tomb) and the same sounds (heavy scratching). It certainly freaked me out.'

Sandy Hager

'Two pictures that I took in the Covenanters' Prison had "orbs" on them. However, the strangest thing happened when we got back to our hotel room. My wife had 5 or 6 large scratch marks on her back, like she had been clawed by something. They were in a "v" shape. The next morning they were completely gone.'

Richard Torble

'I suddenly began to cry and feel an overwhelming feeling of sadness. The closer we got the worse I became and I was sobbing so hard I was almost unable to breathe. It was the most awful feeling of sadness, grief and despair that I have ever felt. I have never cried like that before in my whole life and never want to again.'

Kathryn, Sheffield

'One of our friends was standing next to me in the Black Mausoleum and started hyperventilating about two minutes into us being there. He told me he had seen a ghost inside. He'd actually looked him in the face. He described him as a man with blue eyes and a cloak. He said he felt the most sad and then the most scared he has ever felt in his life. He felt incredibly cold from the inside – the cold sensation had started in his feet and worked its way up through his body.'

Name withheld

'I still felt quite happy when we entered the Covenanters' Prison. It wasn't until I got into the Black Mausoleum itself that I began to feel uneasy. I felt that someone or something was looking right at me. As I turned to look I saw what can only be described as a hooded figure with a featureless face and a couple of inches shorter than me.'

B Johnson, Coventry

'I was standing just inside the crypt and my feet just froze, they went completely numb and I felt a freeze climb my legs. I had to keep stepping from side to side, moving out of the cold spot, but it followed me as I moved around. Later when I stepped back inside so I could have a picture taken I felt a burning sensation on my neck. I noticed my mate was totally pale. He finally asked if I felt anything strange and I described what I felt. He said that, at the time of the photo being taken, he saw a halo that *appeared around my neck and shoulders. He then looked at the back of my neck and noticed it was all red and scratched.'*

Alan Smith

'. . . the next morning after the tour my girlfriend found a series of scratches on her chest. They were very red and fine, quite angry-looking. From memory there were at least three main scratches (each consisting of three to four scratch lines), perhaps more. They certainly weren't done by human hand as they were too close together, more like a tiny cat's paw. The scratches were long too, trailing up to 30–40 centimetres in length.'

Alan Maxwell

'As I was entering the "prison" a woman next to me took a photo. When the flash went off there was what I would describe as a ghost. It was a young girl (maybe 8 or 9 years of age) and she was just standing in front of this tree in what looked like a white or a white lace dress . . . I only wish it showed up on the digital camera but of course it didn't.'

Dan Dickens

'One of the tour party commented to one of the team that she could see "a black mass" in the rear corner of the Mausoleum. Interestingly the EMF [Electronic Voice Phenomena] showed a large rise in activity in the area where the mass was seen. When the person said she could no longer see it, the readings dropped back to normal. A separate team member was approached and told by another tour party member that she had been touched on the back of the neck . . . however, no one was behind her at the time. Another mentioned that he was experiencing numbness in his feet and pins and needles down one side, and yet another reported seeing "rapidly moving lights" on the wall. Sam also reports being scratched

by something across her right hand, but inside her clothes, not through them!'

UK Paranormal Investigator

'We're never going in there again. Ever.'

William Jones

Other visitors complained of feeling gripped around the ankles by an ice-cold band as if they were experiencing what it had felt like to be shackled to the wall in the Covenanters' Prison. Dozens reported that their cameras malfunctioned in certain sites but not in others, while those who managed to capture images of floating balls of light and luminous shapes sent copies to the tour agency and to magazines to prove their claims.

GHOST TOURS

There are currently six separate tour operators offering guided ghost walks of the city and they are all doing a roaring trade. Evidently Edinburgh is a city of spirits and not all of them are bottled. I caught up with Jan-Andrew Henderson, author of the most comprehensive book on haunted Edinburgh, entitled *Edinburgh – City of the Dead*. He is also the founder of the appropriately named Black Hart Tours.

Jan-Andrew (right) once lived in the midst of haunted Edinburgh in a house on the edge of Greyfriars Graveyard and he became fascinated by the history and the distinctive atmosphere of the place. Dissatisfied with the sensationalistic nature of other books on the subject and frustrated by the lack of credible evidence, he decided to trace as many eyewitnesses as he could and record first hand the stories of people who had taken his tour and who claimed to have had a brush with the shadow people.

Jan-Andrew Henderson.

How did your fascination with Edinburgh's hidden history, if I can call it that, begin?

Like many locals, I didn't have a huge interest in Edinburgh history – or any sort of history – until I got a job as a tour guide. Then, because I wanted to be good at it, I began to dig up little-known things and fascinating facts about Edinburgh's past. Then Scotland's past. Now I love all kinds of history, especially the little-known stuff.

What is the legend behind the Black Mausoleum and the Mackenzie poltergeist?

Because I run a walking tour, the area we cover isn't very large, so we stick mainly to the Royal Mile. It was the heart of Edinburgh for thousands of years, and so every inch has history. The Black Mausoleum and the Mackenzie poltergeist are different. The poltergeist has only appeared in the last seven years, so it doesn't have much of a legend. People think it is the ghost of George Mackenzie, but there's actually no evidence for that. It's called the Mackenzie poltergeist because the first reported attack took place on the steps of George Mackenzie's tomb. But most of the attacks after that took place in a fairly nondescript tomb, which is now known as the Black Mausoleum.

The Black Mausoleum seems to differ from Edinburgh's other haunted locations for two reasons. One is the frequency of the poltergeist sightings. The other is the severity of the incidents. The period between the first recorded sightings in 1999 and the present has seen over 350 documented 'attacks' in the Black Mausoleum and Covenanters' Prison. Of these attacks, an astonishing 150 have caused the witness to collapse.

There have been sightings of a white figure, unexplained smells and auditory anomalies – including knocking noises under the ground and inside the tomb itself. Dead animals are found, unmarked, in front of the Black Mausoleum. The area has been exorcized twice – both times unsuccessfully.

King's Advocate George Mackenzie was the scourge of the Covenanters. He doesn't seem to be resting on his laurels: his alleged ghost is one of the best-documented poltergeists ever.

Poltergeist activity has been reported in four different houses around the graveyard and a large fire broke out in the residences behind George Mackenzie's tomb in 2002.

I don't know what the Mackenzie poltergeist really is. I don't know if it's a supernatural entity, a pheromone cloud, a demon or a set of psychosomatic and hysterical reactions. All have been suggested. But I know it has become the best-documented supernatural case of all time and probably the most conclusive.

Let me put it this way – if the Mackenzie poltergeist isn't a genuine supernatural entity then I don't think there's any such thing. Not anywhere in the world.

What manner of experiences have been reported?
Hot spots. Cold spots. People overcome with sorrow. People feeling suddenly nauseous. People are punched, pushed, bitten, burned and have their hair and clothes pulled by something they can't see. Often they feel something under layers of clothes. All have marks to prove it. People falling unconscious. Cameras failing to work. Strange sounds and smells. Auditory anomalies. Spectral voices. One or two people have claimed to be temporarily possessed. Others find the disturbances continue back at their hotel or home. Many feel nothing at all and then discover marks on their body when they leave the tomb.

Have you been unnerved by the experiences that have been reported to you or by the atmosphere of the place? And what effect did it have on you living in proximity to the graveyard? Or have you become immune over time? Your attitude seems to be a challenge to it to show itself.
I've never been unnerved by it. I think it's great. I'm deeply sceptical of traditional 'ghosts' and feel sure there is a rational explanation – even

if I don't have one. But I find the things that happen in the graveyard fascinating rather than scary. I was actually quite surprised that living next to a graveyard with such a haunted reputation didn't faze me. Maybe that's why I'm so determined to be sceptical. If I really did think the place contained a violent supernatural entity, I'd probably find it hard to turn off the lights at night.

What was the most disturbing and convincing case that you have heard about or experienced connected with the City of the Dead?
I've heard many eyewitness accounts, seen the strange marks and witnessed people collapse. But the most convincing thing I saw involved an animal. I saw a bird sitting on the grass just outside the Black Mausoleum, staring into the tomb. It was so transfixed it let me walk right up, kneel beside it and even touch it. It simply refused to take its eyes off the tomb entrance – though it was broad daylight and I could see there was nothing inside. Assuming it couldn't fly, because it was young or injured, I stood up and stepped back. As I did the bird shot backwards, almost as if it had been kicked.

Then it twisted in the air and flew off. I have never seen an animal act that way. And unlike any incident involving a human, it simply couldn't be faked. Something in that empty tomb terrified it to the point where it couldn't move.

Have you seen the bruises, bites, scratches and other injuries that people claim to have sustained during the tour?
I have, because I used to be a tour guide. I also have a number of pictures – though not nearly as many as I should have.

In October 2003 my house overlooking the graveyard burned down, destroying most of my records. I lost five years' worth of letters, photographs, records and statements concerning the Mackenzie poltergeist as well as every possession I had in the world. None of the surrounding properties were damaged and an official cause for the fire has not been established. Fortunately, I had saved most of the sightings and eyewitness accounts on a computer in another building – about the only thing that did survive. I live somewhere else now.

You devised a test to weed out spurious claims. Can you describe that please?
We've tried different things. Taking people into the wrong tomb or describing a fictional 'symptom' of the poltergeist attack to see if people then claim it has happened to them. Unfortunately, there's no foolproof test that anyone can devise.

If there really is a poltergeist, there's no reason such an entity couldn't take its cue from us and move tombs or do exactly what we're describing.

Have psychic mediums ever been on the tour and if so, did they claim to have been able to identify the restless spirit responsible for these phenomena?
We've had lots and they described different things. One or two have sensed children and another couple, a tall figure. Most, however, simply claim to sense a presence that is powerful and malevolent.

What has been your impression of the 'witnesses' you interviewed? Were they genuinely shaken? Were they credible?
Again, there has been a huge range. Some seem far too gullible or just plain weird to be taken seriously. But there are others I simply couldn't imagine making stuff up or being over-imaginative. Sensible, intelligent older men and women, who don't even believe in the paranormal.

Despite your own experiences, such as the inexplicable fire at your former home and having taken the witness statements, you remain unconvinced. Is that true, or is it that you reserve judgement and don't want to put a name to something you haven't seen with your own eyes? Pretty much the latter. That's just the kind of person I am.

I don't believe in God for the same reason – no matter how many people tell me they've been touched by Him. I want empirical evidence before I say: 'Yes, that's a supernatural entity.' The problem is I haven't got empirical evidence for any other explanation. But something odd is certainly going on there.

GHOSTS OF EDINBURGH – THE OLD TOWN

Jan-Andrew kindly offered to act as our tour guide of Edinburgh's Old Town.

The following entries are taken from his definitive guide, *Edinburgh – City of the Dead* (Black and White Publishing) and these are reprinted by kind permission of the publishers.

EDINBURGH CASTLE

The castle is haunted by several apparitions. This is hardly surprising given its history of conflict and the fact that there has been some sort of fortification on Castle Rock since prehistory.

John Graham of Claverhouse, Viscount Dundee, is said to haunt the castle. He was known as 'Bloody Clavers' because of his ruthless persecution of Covenanters in the 17th century – along with his accomplice 'Bloody' George Mackenzie.

When James II of Scotland was deposed, Claverhouse made a momentous about-turn and raised a Catholic highland army to fight for his king. He was killed leading a magnificent highland charge at the Battle of Killiekrankie in

The Old Town of Edinburgh.

1689 and, because of this is better known in Scots lore as 'Bonny' Dundee. He was first seen in the castle on the night of his death by Lord Balcarres, who was in charge of the castle's Jacobite prisoners, and has appeared periodically from then on.

That same year the Duke of Gordon, governor of the castle, stabbed his steward for bringing news of his family's death. The unfortunate man now wanders the walls. Some employees are just impossible to get rid of.

The castle, it seems, is afflicted with all sorts of military-themed spooks. Phantom drumming was first heard in 1650 and the castle was taken by Oliver Cromwell's forces soon after – leading to the idea that this was a portent for disaster. In later sightings the drummer is sometimes invisible, sometimes headless and was last reported in the 1960s.

The ramparts also boast ghostly bagpiping and the invisible marching of massed men. The dungeons are said to be plagued by the ghosts of prisoners held during the Napoleonic Wars and blue orbs have been captured on film.

The castle is also haunted by Janet Douglas, Lady Glamis. A member of the Douglas family, long distrusted by the Stuart kings, she was accused of witchcraft on a trumped-up charge and burned at the stake in 1537 in front of her husband and son. A busy ghost, she also manages to find time to haunt Glamis Castle in Angus.

THE LAWNMARKET

Site of Edinburgh's last public hanging in 1864. There is a legend of a Marie Celeste-style house here. In the 18th century one of the flats was suddenly abandoned in panic, right in the middle of a dinner party. The exit was so hasty that half-eaten food was left on the table, though those who fled did lock the door behind them – a door that was never reopened. I must admit this bit of the legend puzzles me. If the door was never unlocked again, how do we know what was left on the table?

By the 19th century the story had passed into lore with Robert Chambers

The imposing edifice of Edinburgh Castle – ghostly piping and the sound of marching can be heard on the ramparts.

writing, 'No one knows to whom the house belongs; no one ever inquires after it, no one living ever saw the inside of it, it is a condemned house.' Unfortunately it really was condemned and no longer exists.

CITY CHAMBERS, ROYAL MILE

Underneath are the remains of Mary King's Close, the famous haunted street.

THE SCOTSMAN HOTEL, NORTH BRIDGE

Formerly the Scotsman *newspaper office, which seemed to have a whole plethora of ghosts. In 1990 a security guard ran into an employee who he knew to be dead. In 1994 a page-make-up artist, working in the basement, came across a door he had never seen before. Upon entering he stumbled upon a phantom printer sporting old-fashioned clothes and beard and carrying antiquated printing plates. The building was also haunted by a blonde woman who would vanish any time a member of staff came over to ask what she wanted. Apparently, there is also a phantom forger. Then again, you can't believe everything you read in the press.*

THE SOUTH BRIDGE

Vaults inside the bridge are said to be haunted by a faceless man and a mischievous poltergeist.

WHISTLE BINKIE'S BAR, NIDDRY STREET

This bar, refashioned out of 19th-century converted bridge vaults, is haunted by a long-haired gentleman in 17th-century attire. He is called 'the Watcher' but no one has ever seen his face. This bar and the storerooms of South Bridge shops are also home to an entity known as 'the Imp'. This mischievous creature stops clocks, slams doors and moves objects. Sightings began in the early 1990s and continue to this day.

ST MARY'S STREET

Haunted by the victim of an apparently motiveless murder. A young woman was killed here in 1916 by an assailant who leapt out of a doorway, stabbed her and ran off, without robbing her or molesting her in any other way. She is still seen occasionally, her clothes splattered with blood, an understandably astonished expression on her face.

THE MUSEUM OF CHILDHOOD, ROYAL MILE

The area behind this building is said to ring with the voices of crying children late at night. During the plague years, an outbreak occurred in a nearby nursery, which was sealed up with the children and mothers inside.

CHESSELS COURT

Site of Deacon Brodie's last botched robbery at the Edinburgh Excise Office. In the late 19th century, the tenements that stand there were haunted by a woman wearing a black silk veil – identified as an occupant who had recently hanged herself.

THE CANONGATE, ROYAL MILE

Haunted by a burning woman. She was the daughter of an influential family in the 18th century but had the misfortune to fall pregnant by a servant. A minister was called to deliver the last rites to the girl, which he objected to, since she looked perfectly healthy. He was given money and threatened to keep his mouth shut.

Later that day the girl was killed when an 'accidental' fire mysteriously burned the house down. The house was rebuilt but caught fire again many years later.

In the heart of the conflagration the girl appeared, screaming, 'Once burnt, twice burnt, the third time I'll scare you all!' The third fire has, so far, not occurred.

QUEENSBURY HOUSE, CANONGATE

Haunted by a kitchen boy who was roasted and eaten by James Douglas, the lunatic Earl of Drumlanrig – son of the Duke of Queensbury. At the time the Duke was arranging the union of Scottish and English parliaments in 1707 – an act so loathed by the Edinburgh people that they rioted in the streets and cursed his house.

HOLYROOD PALACE, ROYAL MILE

This has an excellent class of ghost – being haunted by Mary Queen of Scots, her husband Lord Darnley and her secretary David Rizzio – all of whom came to violent ends. Lowering the tone is the naked ghost of Bald Agnes, who was stripped and tortured in 1592 after being accused of witchcraft.

THE COWGATE

Site of the 'Cleansing of the Causeway' in 1524 – Scotland's largest street fight in which hundreds of participants were killed. The Cowgate was the birthplace of Walter Scott and James Connolly, the Irish republican leader. The area is haunted by an unnamed man with rope burns round his neck.

WEST BOW (VICTORIA STREET)

Anderson's Close, demolished in 1827, was the home of Major Thomas Weir (The Wizard of the West Bow). It was also 'Stinking Close' and after repeated sightings of spectres came to be known as 'Haunted Close'.

The West Bow is also haunted by a phantom coach and the ghost of a sailor named Angus Roy. Crippled on a voyage in 1820, he settled in this area and spent the next twenty years there until his death. He longed for the sea and was tormented by local children who mimicked his severe limp. He is still seen occasionally, dragging his injured leg behind him. It's a shame he picked such a steep street to haunt.

GRASSMARKET

This was the site where Covenanters were executed and a circular monument set into the ground commemorates these tragic events. It was also the place of public hangings and the cleverly named Last Drop pub is behind the spot.

The White Hart Inn, where the mass murderers William Burke and William Hare reputedly picked up victims in the 1820s, still stands here.

The area is haunted by a woman with a burned face and the phantom coach that gallops down the West Bow sometimes carries on through the Grassmarket.

BELL'S WYND

In 1780 a tenant in one of the tenements, George Gourly, repeatedly approached his landlord with what he thought was a reasonable request. His family was growing and he wished to rent the empty flat below his.

His landlord Patrick Guthrie always said no, but refused to give a reason for the rebuttal. In frustration Gourlay broke into the flat and found a ghostly female figure standing in the middle of the room. He was so frightened that he reported what he had done to the procurator fiscal. An

The White Hart Inn the Grassmarket was where mass murderers William Burke and William Hare reputedly picked up victims.

investigation discovered the corpse of Patrick Guthrie's wife in the empty flat. He had killed her when he found out she'd been having an affair.

GEORGE IV BRIDGE

Number 21 is 'The Elephant House' where Harry Potter and the Philosopher's Stone *was written.*

Bridge vaults under the National Library of Scotland are haunted by an unidentified highland chief. When he was spotted by librarian Elizabeth Clarke in 1973, she noticed that his hands were manacled. The bridge vaults were used in the 19th century to imprison debtors.

BEDLAM THEATRE, FOREST ROAD

Near the site of a former asylum. Haunted by a shadowy figure that flits through the theatre.

CHAPTER THREE

ANGELS AND APPARITIONS

The vengeful ghost has become a cliché of graphic horror fiction and films. But in reality it seems that a restless spirit can do little more than appear looking melancholic and hope that it will prick the conscience of the guilty party into making a full confession, or persuade a kindly soul to restore its reputation. Ghosts have also been known to warn of danger and even to take control of endangered ships and aircraft, guiding their pilots and passengers to safety.

ACCUSED FROM BEYOND THE GRAVE

In January 1897 Mary Jane Heaster of Greenbrier, West Virginia was grieving for her daughter Zona who had died in mysterious circumstances earlier that month at the age of 23. The official cause of death was recorded as being 'complications resulting from childbirth', but Mary Jane was adamant that her daughter had not been pregnant. Zona had, in fact, given birth to an illegitimate child two years earlier, but it was preposterous to suggest that her health had been compromised to such an extent that she could have succumbed as a result.

Mary Jane was not satisfied. Her suspicions had been further aroused by the testimony of the attending physician, Dr Knapp, who was also, coincidentally, the coroner. He had been summoned to Zona's home on the fateful night to find that her husband of just three months, Edward (Erasmus) Shue, had moved the body to an upstairs bedroom and had re-dressed her in her finest Sunday clothes.

He was in a severely agitated state, cradling his new bride's lifeless body in his arms and wailing as melodramatically as a music hall villain. He refused to allow the doctor to examine her closely, insisting that he be left in peace to grieve. He claimed to know nothing of the circumstances that had led to her death as the body had been discovered by a young boy whom he had sent to the house on an errand. It was the boy who had found her lying lifeless downstairs and had run for help.

All Edward would say was that she had succumbed to an 'everlasting fit'. Under the circumstances Dr Knapp could do nothing more than catch a cursory glimpse of the dead woman's face which he observed had a marked discolouration on the right cheek and on the neck consistent with a blow and strangulation.

At the wake Edward's erratic behaviour aroused further suspicion. He refused to allow any of the mourners to approach the casket and had covered the marks on her neck with a scarf which he claimed had been her favourite.

Zona's ghost revealed how she had suffered at the hands of her abusive husband.

It was quite by chance that her mother happened to remove a white sheet from the coffin just before the burial. Perhaps it was female intuition or a whisper from beyond the grave. Whatever compelled her to recover the sheet it was to prove a defining moment in the case.

THE INDELIBLE STAIN

The first thing Mary Jane noticed was the odd odour which she had initially attributed to embalming fluid, but the more familiar she became with that smell, the more convinced she became that it was something else, something indefinable. When she tried to rinse the sheet the water turned the colour of blood. Scooping some of it out with a jug she was astonished to see it was as clear as drinking water, yet the water in the bowl remained crimson red. The sheet was no longer white, but pink, the colour of diluted blood.

No matter how hard she scrubbed the sheet and no matter how long she soaked it, the stubborn stain remained. The only thing Mary Jane could do now was pray. She demanded answers, for if denied she knew she would lose her mind from grief. In the following days when the dying light of day had receded and the shadows lengthened her prayers were answered.

On four successive nights Zona's earthbound spirit manifested in her mother's house and revealed how she had suffered at the hands of her abusive husband. On the night of 22 January he had flown into a rage when he learned that she hadn't cooked meat for his dinner. He beat her and broke her neck. And to prove it, the apparition turned its head around 360 degrees! Had anyone inspected the body they would have seen the incriminating bruising and felt the dislocated vertebra in the neck. But as no post mortem had been performed there was no evidence to support the mother's suspicions, other than the accusation of a ghost.

EXHUMATION

Nevertheless Mary Jane marched over to the office of the local prosecutor, John Alfred Preston, and demanded that he put the question to her former son-in-law. Preston couldn't order Edward's arrest on hearsay evidence at the best of times and certainly not on that allegedly provided by a ghost. But he had his doubts concerning Edward's version of events and was only too willing to have Zona's body exhumed for an autopsy. Edward's evident distress at the news seemed to confirm what everyone in the town had been saying for weeks – that he had taken her life and, therefore, he couldn't be permitted to get away with it.

The autopsy confirmed that the real cause of death was strangulation which was all the prosecutor needed to instigate proceedings. Edward was immediately arrested and while he paced up and down his tiny cell in the county jail further investigations unearthed his chequered past. Proof was obtained of two earlier marriages, one of which ended in divorce and the other with the 'accidental' death of the second wife who had been killed by a blow to the head. Apparently three wives were not enough for Edward, who boasted to his fellow inmates that he intended to chalk up seven marriage partners before he settled down to an ignominious old age. He was confident that no jury would convict him. After all, what evidence could they have? No one had actually seen him murder his wife. An intruder could have done it. All he needed to do was sow sufficient reasonable doubt and he'd walk out of the courtroom a free man.

He had heard rumours of Zona's ghost, but dismissed it out of hand as the ravings of a grief-stricken mother. Unfortunately for the prosecution, testimony pertaining to the ghost was ruled inadmissible by the judge even before the trial got under way. When Edward walked into the courtroom on the first day of the trial it was all he could do to suppress a smug grin.

THE TRIAL

Edward's attorney shared his client's over-confidence and that was his undoing. He thought he would have some fun at Mary Jane's expense by asking her to repeat her ghost story in the belief that it would discredit her in the eyes of the jury. But she remained calm throughout the questioning, impressing both the jury and the judge. Nothing the defence could say seemed to sway her. It was not her imagination, she assured the court, that had told her that her daughter had been killed by having her breath choked out of her and her neck 'squeezed off at the first vertebra'. That was the first time that the precise cause of death had been mentioned during the proceedings and when it was subsequently confirmed by the physician who had written the autopsy report there was a hushed silence in the courtroom. Edward was caught in a web of deceit and subsequently convicted of murder. The only reason he escaped execution was the fact that he had been convicted on circumstantial evidence and not the word of an eyewitness. He died in prison on 13 March 1900 and is the only man to have been convicted of murder in the United States on the testimony of a ghost.

THE PHANTOM PILOT

In the autumn of 1916 a flight training school in Montrose, Scotland was the scene of a series of hauntings which seem to support the belief that a spirit will return from the world beyond if it feels compelled to right a wrong or seek recognition it believes it deserves.

For several months a vaguely discernible figure attired in a pilot's uniform was seen outside the mess hall by senior members of staff. It would approach the door of the hut then vanish. Inside meanwhile, pilots and staff would describe having sensed a presence. One even swore that he saw the spectre standing at the foot of his bed. Subsequent research concluded that the ghost must have been that of flight instructor Desmond Arthur who had been killed during a routine flight in 1913 as the result of a botched repair to his biplane. The error had apparently been covered up and the accident attributed to pilot error which must have had Arthur spinning in his grave, for as soon as the true facts came to light, the haunting ceased and Arthur presumably returned to his rightful resting place.

THE DOOMED U-BOAT

On a darker note, the crew of German submarine UB-65 appear to have been doomed from the moment their U-boat was built. During its first voyage a torpedo exploded while being loaded aboard, killing six men and the second officer. But this was not the last time the officer was seen aboard. While it was on its first patrol the crew reported seeing the officer standing on deck with his arms folded and looking up into the clouds. He was seen again the day the captain was killed and thereafter whenever some disaster struck the vessel. The mere appearance of the phantom was sufficient to drive one sailor into committing suicide by jumping into the sea although nothing untoward had actually occurred that day. On its final fateful voyage in 1918 it was sighted apparently abandoned on the surface by a US submarine, L-2, whose captain ordered his crew to action stations in the belief that it was a trap. But before he could fire on it the U-boat exploded and sank beneath the waves. The last thing the American captain noted in his log was the appearance of a German officer standing motionless on the hull, his arms folded and looking upwards into the sky.

GHOST SHIPS

Such incidents are often attributed to echoes in the ether, but there have been many cases where ghosts have actively intervened to save the living. In 1949 the captain of the passenger liner *Port Pirie* was on shore in Sydney, Australia awaiting orders while the crew were giving the ship a last look over in preparation for their next voyage.

One of the engineers filled the boiler and turned the pumps off when the gauge indicated that the boiler was full. But as he walked away the pumps started up by themselves. After double-checking the gauge he turned the pumps off again and turned away, but again the pumps turned themselves back on. Now that his curiosity had been aroused he stripped down the boiler and gave it a thorough overhaul. He discovered that the gauge was faulty and had been registering that the boiler was full when it was almost empty.

Had the ship been allowed to sail with this fault undetected it could have resulted in a fatal explosion at sea with the loss of all hands. When the engineer told his crewmates about this one of them remembered that it had happened before. The ship's first chief engineer had been killed after the boiler had run dry and blown up. With his last breath he had vowed that he would never let it happen again. Could he have been responsible for turning the boiler pump back on to warn his successor of the potentially fatal fault?

A similar story surrounds the sinking of the sailing ship the *Pamir*, which sank in the Atlantic in 1957 with very few survivors. Since then this modern Flying Dutchman has been sighted by several ships in distress whose crews reported being saved from certain death by the phantom ship.

Although the *Pamir* does not appear to have taken an active part in the rescue of the stricken ships, the grateful survivors swear that it exerted a 'mysterious force' which pulled them out of a squall into calmer seas while remaining unaffected by the bad weather itself. Such seamen's stories may seem far-fetched, but it is worth noting that the rescued seamen mentioned that one of the phantom ship's crew could clearly be seen with his arm in a sling – a fact that was only later confirmed by one of the *Pamir*'s surviving crew members.

An interesting footnote to the *Pamir* case is that every time it has been sighted its crew are fewer in number, suggesting that with every rescue the curse is lifted for one or more of its doomed sailors.

THE PHANTOM PILOT

By no means all ghosts are out for revenge or to right an injustice. Some appear to be guardian angels in disguise. One of the most remarkable cases was that reported by British pilot Bill Corfield, who flew into a terrible thunderstorm en route to Athens in 1947. As the plane and its crew were buffeted by high winds and visibility was severely reduced, Bill had little choice but to take them down to 20 metres above sea level and fly blind in the hope of breaking through the clouds.

Just then his navigator spotted the Corinth Canal, an extremely narrow passage only 5 metres wider than the wing of the plane. Instinctively Bill banked into the mouth of the canal and levelled off, flying in the pitch dark for 7 kilometres, a manoeuvre Bill later admitted was 'suicidal'.

But no one panicked. In fact, the crew were overwhelmed by a sense of serenity one compared to being in a cathedral. Bill admitted, 'I knew – absolutely and without doubt – that my brother [Jimmy, who had been killed in World War Two] was with me in the aircraft. There was nothing physical [to see] but he was there.'

So convinced was he of his brother's presence that Bill took his hands off the steering controls and let his brother pilot the plane. It was only when they were clear of the canal and in clear skies that

Bill took back control and delivered the plane and its grateful crew to their destination.

THE LAST FLIGHT

Ghost ships have long been a staple ingredient of salty sea tales and ghost trains are said to have been sighted on more than one abandoned railway line, but phantom planes are a distinct rarity.

Early on the morning of 13 June 1993 air traffic controllers at John Wayne airport, in Orange County south of Los Angeles, were besieged by calls from pilots complaining that a private plane was invading their airspace, posing a serious risk to both inbound and outgoing aircraft.

Its shrill engine sent three noise monitors into the red and annoyed the ground staff who noted its FAA (Federal Aviation Administration) number so they could lodge a formal complaint. People living in the exclusive properties surrounding the airport had also been driven to distraction.

They'd been phoning the authorities all morning to voice their anger that a maverick pilot was being allowed to disrupt their breakfast, buzzing their homes and performing aerobatics too near to a residential area.

In fact, he had been flying so low that several irate citizens had noted the FAA number painted on the distinctive red fuselage: N21X. Within the hour the registered owner had been identified.

It was Donald 'Deke' Slayton, a former Mercury astronaut, captain of the 1975 Apollo-Soyuz mission who was known to have an insatiable appetite for speed.

NOBODY'S HERO

But he was nobody's hero that morning. As his plane finally climbed into the clouds and faded from the radar screens muttered curses

Ghost ships have long been a staple of salty sea tales, ghost trains have been sighted on more than one abandoned railway line, but phantom planes are a rarity.

and annoyance was all that trailed in his wake. It was not only a damn nuisance, it was a highly irresponsible stunt and more than a few residents were determined to pursue their complaint through the FAA until they got a result. It wasn't long in coming.

Two weeks later a letter of censure against 'Deke' Slayton was approved and three weeks after that it was finally delivered to his wife Bobbie.

Only she wasn't his wife any longer. When she called the FAA to ask them what kind of sick joke they thought they were playing she made it very clear indeed that she was Deke's widow and she was angry with good reason. She had been with him that morning at his bedside hundreds of miles away in Texas as he lay dying from brain cancer.

And no, no one else could have borrowed the plane as it was on display in an aeronautics museum in Nevada on the day in question, stripped of its engine.

CHAPTER FOUR

BACK FROM THE DEAD

Some of the best evidence of the soul's survival after death has been obtained from mediums, acutely sensitive or psychic individuals who claim to be able to contact the dead. In rare cases they have been able to produce physical manifestations of the deceased which investigators were able to question at length and even to touch, confirming that their presence was not a hoax, nor the product of hypnotic suggestion.

> *'I cannot but think that it would be a great step if mankind could familiarise themselves with the idea that they are spirits incorporated for a time in the flesh; but that the dissolution of the connection between soul and body, though it changes the external condition of the former, leaves its moral state unaltered. What a man has made himself he will be; his state is the result of his past life, and his heaven or hell is in himself.'*

CATHERINE CROWE, *The Night Side of Nature*, 1848

Psychics were once seen by the general public as eccentric and highly unstable individuals and many were exposed as charlatans who cynically exploited the bereaved for monetary gain, but fortunately the recent success of films such as *The Sixth Sense* and the TV series *Medium* have popularized the idea that ordinary people can communicate with the dead to bring comfort and closure to the grief-stricken and that ghosts are a natural and not a supernatural phenomenon.

Many of today's celebrity psychics such as Britain's Derek Acorah, Colin Fry and Tony Stockwell and American TV mediums John Edward and James Van Praagh saw their first apparitions when they were very young, when their connection to the spirit world was at its strongest. It was only when others insisted such things were figments of their imaginations that they learned to fear the appearance of ghosts and to deny the evidence of their own eyes to avoid their parents' displeasure and the jeers of other children.

It takes a rare and acute sensitivity to sense the presence of discarnate personalities and a willingness to openly acknowledge their existence in order to communicate with them. Few people choose to develop this innate ability and to accept the responsibility that goes with their 'gift' because it opens a whole 'Pandora's Box' of problems, from being accused of imagining things to being pestered by the dead who are desperate to reassure their loved ones that they have not ceased to exist but are merely living in a parallel dimension.

MIRABELLI'S SÉANCES

In the early years of spiritualism, just prior to and following the First World War, several serious investigations by eminent scientists were hampered by the crude deceptions perpetrated by fraudulent mediums preying on the gullible and the grief-stricken. But not all could be so readily dismissed as fakes. There were some whose demonstrations appear to offer incontrovertible proof of ghosts. The most remarkable medium of this period was without doubt the young Brazilian Carlos Mirabelli, who first attracted public attention in 1919 when he was chosen as the subject of an intense and exhaustive investigation by the Cesare Lombroso Academy of Psychical Studies. During their tests Mirabelli agreed to conduct a series of 392 séances in broad daylight or in well-lit rooms. At one particularly memorable session he brought through the disembodied spirit of a little girl which assumed physical form in full view of the assembled witnesses. One of these, a Dr de Souza, rose slowly to his feet and in a voice quivering with emotion addressed the apparition which was dressed in a funeral shroud. He addressed it by name, certain that it was his little daughter who had recently died from influenza. Unable to contain himself the doctor rushed at the ghost and embraced it. He was seen to converse with it for a full 30 minutes before it melted back into the

Carlo Mirabelli (left, in trance) with Dr Carlos de Castro (right) in the 1920s. Between them is the 'materialization' of dead poet Giuseppe Parini.

ether. Afterwards he testified that it had talked of matters that only his dead daughter could have known.

At another sitting the spirit of a bishop who had lost his life at sea materialized for more than 20 minutes, during which a physician examined it and noted the rumblings of its stomach and the saliva in its mouth.

Fortunately, someone had the presence of mind to bring a camera to one of the subsequent sessions, during which Mirabelli conjured a robed figure who was sufficiently solid to cast a shadow and leave his image for all time on film. But such feats were sadly ignored by the public whose fascination for phenomena and need to believe had been cruelly exploited by a number of well-publicized scandals involving fraudulent mediums.

MESSAGE FROM THE OTHER SIDE

Although many mediums pass on seemingly mundane messages from the dear departed which don't add a jot to our knowledge of the great beyond, there are others who appear to be able to help in very practical ways.

More recently English housewife Brenda Richardson was still mourning her recently deceased husband Charles when she was invited to a Spiritualist Church by a friend who thought it might offer her a crumb of comfort. Spiritualist meetings always feature a 'platform' medium who takes to the stage after the service to convey messages from the dead to their loved ones in the congregation.

Brenda was not a believer but her interest was aroused when the medium taking the meeting told her that she had a message from Charles who was standing next to her at that very moment. He wanted his widow to know that a painting he had bought and hung in their dining room had not been bought on a whim, as he had told

Psychic photo taken by Dr Thadeu de Mederios on the instruction of Mirabelli. This features a deceased Englishwoman called Zabelle, complete with Mirabellian 'radiations'.

her at the time, but as an investment and now was the time to sell it. It would solve her financial worries. Brenda had not told anyone of her money problems and she hadn't given a thought to the painting, which didn't appear to be in any way remarkable. But the medium was insistent. The painting was valuable. The artist's name was W.H. Davies and his signature was to be found in the bottom right-hand corner of the canvas. Rushing home, Brenda didn't wait to take her shoes and coat off but burst into the living room and almost pulled the picture off the wall. There in the bottom right-hand corner, as the medium had told her, was the artist's signature 'W.H. Davies' – a comparatively obscure but highly respected 19th-century English artist. The painting was subsequently put up for auction and realized a sum that solved Brenda's money troubles at a stroke.

TALKING TO THE DEAD

Most of us would consider it extraordinary if we saw a ghost once in our lives, but there are people who see them every day. In fact, they sometimes have difficulty distinguishing the living from the dead. These psychically-gifted individuals are commonly called clairvoyants (meaning 'clear-sighted'), but many prefer to be called 'sensitives' for fear of being associated with fairground fortune tellers and the kind of eccentric old ladies who gave mediumship a bad reputation in the dark days of spiritualism and séances. Today's mediums are more likely to be ageing hippies offering spiritual guidance at new age fairs or young celebrity psychics with their own TV shows who give readings live on air in front of an enthralled studio audience.

Like many of his contemporaries, American TV psychic James Van Praagh was extremely reluctant to answer his 'calling', but was persuaded to put his gift to good use when the ghosts of several murdered children appealed to him to catch their killer.

Medium and psychic James Van Praagh – 'only certain people are sensitive enough to act as mediums'.

The first victim had attempted to make contact when James was still a child, but he had been terrified by the appearance of the boy at his window at night and had prayed for the persistent phantom to leave him alone. His fear was aggravated by his parents' anger with what they thought was their son's morbid imagination. James later learnt that his mother's aversion to such stories stemmed from her own psychic experiences and the abilities which she had chosen to suppress because it conflicted with her strict Catholic upbringing. Unfortunately, she sent her son to a Catholic school where his 'gifts' brought him even more trouble.

One day he 'saw' a young girl in the playground carrying a pair of ice skates. James had the impression that she wanted to tell her brother that he was not to blame himself for her death which had occurred when she had fallen through the ice, but when James tried to tell his classmate that his dead sister had a message for him the boy flew into a rage and complained to the head of the school who branded James a fantasist and a liar. Things got worse later that same day when James warned his teacher that her son was going to be hit by a car but survive with a broken leg. That night she came to James' home to tell him that his prediction had come true, but she warned him that such 'gifts' were bestowed by the Devil.

MEETING 'EDDIE'

But the Devil couldn't have sent him the next vision. During a school outing to a local nature reserve, James met a boy in the forest who was the same age as himself and who was holding a pet turtle as if it was his only friend. The boy said that his name was Eddie, and James felt a bond with him which he put down to the fact that they were both outsiders.

But there was something about him that was not quite right. Eddie had an unfashionable haircut and wore hand-me-down clothes that a kid might have had in the 1940s or 1950s. He also had an air of melancholy about him which James attributed to the fact that he was wearing a leg brace that must have prevented him from playing with other children. When James started walking back to his group he turned to say goodbye but Eddie was gone. Soon after, the knocking at James' bedroom window began again, only this time the terrified child could see the face of the person who demanded to be let in. It was Eddie. As soon as he put the light on the vision vanished and James realized that Eddie was a ghost.

As a result, James prayed even harder to be spared the visits from the spirits and the visions eventually ceased.

I SEE DEAD PEOPLE

It was only in middle age that the memories James had so long repressed came back to the surface. By this time he had his own manufacturing business and was looking for someone to design and maintain a website. The lady who answered his advertisement happened to be a psychic who during casual conversation made accurate predictions concerning family matters she couldn't have known by conventional methods. She even described a dream that James had had since the age of six in which he was an adult sitting at his mother's hospital bed when the spirit of his grandmother entered to claim her daughter for the other world.

James was naturally intrigued, but he didn't want anything to do with mediums for fear of awakening his own unwanted talents. 'I've had my fill of the supernatural,' he told her.

Nevertheless, she persisted and managed to persuade him to join her at a psychic demonstration presided over by a local medium she trusted. During the meeting the medium claimed to see James surrounded by dead people desperate to communicate with their loved ones through him. 'You can shut the door to the spirit world if you want to,' he told James, 'but they used to talk to you and they want to talk to you again. They tell me that you have dreamt again of your grandmother. It is the same dream you had when you were six years old. You are in the hospital and your grandmother comes to collect your mother who is dying.'

Dismissing it all as a cruel trick in which his new employee and the medium must have been complicit, James excused himself and left the meeting vowing never to be duped again. But he wasn't to be allowed to squander his gift so easily.

One day he 'saw' his recently deceased mother wandering aimlessly through the aisles at the local supermarket as if searching for something or someone. Before he could follow her a young black boy dropped a pack of eggs at his feet and walked off without a word. As James bent down to clean up the mess he noticed that the name on the packet was 'Mother Hen Nurseries'. It didn't mean anything to him at the time, but it was to prove a vital clue in the mystery of the missing children.

EMPTY NEST

A second enigmatic clue came some time later when James opened his mailbox to find a bird's nest filled with seven blue eggs. Thinking the neighbourhood children were playing a prank he put it aside and thought no more of it. But that same night the black boy he had seen in the supermarket appeared in his living room holding the nest. But this time it was empty and the boy's hands were bound with rope.

James was clearly being asked to rescue an earthbound spirit, but when he asked the boy what he wanted, the child could say nothing. 'Tell me what you want of me,' James repeated, frustrated and somewhat frightened. This time the boy opened his mouth to speak and a stream of soil poured on to the carpet. These visions James was seeing with his inner eye, the so-called 'third eye' of psychic perception.

Suffering from headaches and with his business in serious trouble because of changing economic conditions, James consulted a counsellor, but his sessions provided little comfort. At one particularly memorable session he 'saw' a middle-aged woman burst into the counsellor's office in a highly agitated state and begin ransacking his desk. James couldn't understand why the counsellor failed to react and then he realized it was because he couldn't hear or see her. She was dead. A moment later he understood the significance of what he was seeing. She was the counsellor's late wife and this was a replay of the last moments of her life. James watched helpless as she discovered a bottle of tablets and swallowed the lot, dying right before his eyes. He described what he was seeing, but was cut short by the counsellor who recognized his late wife from the description and refused to hear as much as another word from his 'delusional' patient.

THE OLD MAN

Being psychic does not mean that you are immune from life's trials. Certainly James has had more than his share. Following his mother's death and the loss of his business he had to leave his home and find a more modest house. Some would say that it is these factors and the resulting stress which produced the 'visions', but they cannot explain what happened next.

During a visit to the local police station to report a break-in, he saw the spirit of a troubled old man vainly trying to communicate with his widow who had come in to find out how the police investigation into her husband's death was progressing. Reluctant though he was to intervene and acutely aware that he was likely to be accused of being insane, James felt obliged to pass on the old man's message.

Her son was predictably suspicious of a stranger who claimed to see dead people and over-protective towards his mother, but she was eager to have a last word with her beloved husband if there was any chance that this visitation was true. She had been distraught when he had failed to return home just days before and James was able to break the news that he did not die of a heart attack as the police assumed, but had been mugged when he took a shortcut home. A young man had stolen the watch that her husband had been so proud of together with his wedding ring.

While mention of the watch and ring could be credited to good guesswork, it didn't account for James' knowledge of the place where the old man's body had been found nor the fact that he knew that the old man's ghost had knocked their wedding photo from the shelf while she was dusting that morning.

Although the son managed to have James evicted from the station for harassment, his mother was not so easily put off. She called on James later that day, having found his address from the form he had been filling out at the station about the break-in, and she asked for more information.

Restoring contact with the old man, James was able to give her specific personal details including the number of the hotel room in which they spent their honeymoon. Then James' heightened sense of empathy helped him relive the agony of the old man's last moments – the fear he felt when confronted with the mugger and the pain of his fatal heart attack brought about by the struggle.

From this James was able to give the widow a detailed description of the mugger and the house he shared with his parents. Better still, he told her that the young man was known to the police. In fact, he was a police informant and his first name was Ronnie. James revealed that Ronnie had hidden her husband's watch and ring together with other stolen items in a cigar box under the steps leading to the front porch.

Naturally the police were sceptical and questioned James before deciding whether or not to act on his information. But he was able to convince the female detective assigned to the case that his insights were genuine by telling her precisely where she could find the reading glasses that she had mislaid that morning. The tip proved accurate: Ronnie was arrested and the stolen items were recovered.

PSYCHOMETRIC INSIGHT

But not every message James brought from the beyond was appreciated. When he felt compelled to pass on a message from the detective's dead sister who had died in a car crash years before, she didn't want to hear it and was angry that he had intruded on her private grief. She was clearly uncomfortable with the idea that the dead can haunt the living, but she could not afford to ignore the clues he brought to her regarding Eddie and the other dead children which now began to accumulate thick and fast.

By this time James was working in a bookshop. One day he happened to be wrapping a copy of Edgar Allan Poe's *Collected Tales* when it fell open at an illustration for *The Premature Burial*. Instinctively James realized why the black boy had appeared to him mute and bound. He had been buried alive. Desperate for more details that he could bring to the police, he consulted a Ouija board and asked to be given the name of the boy who had repeatedly appeared holding the bird's nest. Obligingly the board spelt out the name Dennis Branston.

The following day James was driving home when Dennis suddenly appeared in front of him, forcing him to brake suddenly. The next moment the boy was sitting beside him with the nest cupped in his lap. 'What are you trying to tell me?' asked James, more in frustration than in fright. It was then that he noticed where he was – in Bird's Nest Lane. Surely, it couldn't be a coincidence. This had to be Dennis' way of telling James where he had died.

Continuing along the road without his guide James came to Mother Hen Nurseries, the same name that had appeared on the box of eggs Dennis had dropped at his feet in the supermarket. He must be on the right road. Minutes later he pulled into Turtleback Park – the nature reserve where he had met Eddie all those years earlier.

Leaving the car, James wandered through the woods, all the while appealing to the spirits of Eddie and Dennis to make themselves known to him and tell him how he could help bring them peace. He was answered in a way that would send lesser psychics running for cover. One by one the restless spirits of seven dead boys rose from the ground – Eddie, Dennis and five others who had been buried with them.

When the police arrived at the scene they unearthed the bodies of all seven children, their hands bound at the wrists just as James had seen them – all except one. The body of Eddie Katz was recovered, the leg brace still intact – proof if needed that James' insights were genuine. But Eddie's hands were not bound and the autopsy revealed that he had died from a single gunshot wound. Forensic tests showed that he had died many years before the others – 30 years earlier in fact, which coincided with the date of his disappearance in May 1963.

A cold case is the hardest to crack and a case this cold yielded up no forensic evidence of any use at all. When James learnt of this he offered to try to get what impressions he could of the killer from Eddie's leg brace, a technique known as psychometry. Psychics believe that inanimate objects can retain residual personal energy and that it is possible to tune in to the 'memories' stored in an object simply by holding it. Personal possessions such as watches and rings are potentially the most promising material, but any object associated with a strong emotion – such as a murder weapon – can reveal vital information if the psychic is acutely sensitive. With little else to go on the police reluctantly agreed to let James attempt his experiment. To their amazement it yielded the crucial clues they were looking for.

By simply holding the brace James instantly connected with the strongest emotions Eddie had experienced – the moment of his death. For a few vital seconds, James looked out through Eddie's eyes. He was alone in the forest at Turtleback Reserve in the very spot where James had first seen him as a boy all those years ago. Two hunters were stalking deer less than a hundred yards away. One was Lester Petrocelli and the other was his brother Richard. They heard a movement in the undergrowth and believing that they had their prey in their sights Richard shouted to Lester to fire. He hit Eddie in the head and the boy died instantly. When they found the body they panicked and buried it, promising each other never to speak to anyone of what they had done.

On questioning Mrs Katz the police discovered that someone had been sending her flowers every Christmas with a card in his name and that is why she had assumed that her son was still alive. The man had protected his anonymity by paying the florist in cash sent in the mail, but after three decades he must have felt he was in the clear because that Christmas he turned up in person. Asked if she could give the police a description, the florist assured them she wouldn't need to as he was a familiar face in town. He was the man the Revenue

Service used every year on billboards and leaflets in their advertising campaign to remind people to file their income tax returns. His name was Lester Petrocelli.

Ghosts aren't satisfied with haunting a location if they have revenge on their mind. Through our dreams and by influencing our thoughts they can conspire to arrange a meeting that might seem like an uncanny coincidence to the unsuspecting pawns in their play. It can surely be no coincidence that just days later James saw Lester Petrocelli in a local restaurant with the spirit of his recently deceased brother Richard standing behind him urging James to convey a vital message from beyond the grave.

'Excuse me,' James interrupted as politely as he could. 'I don't know how to tell you this so I'm just going to say it. Your brother is standing behind you and he says you are not to blame yourself for the death of the boy even though you pulled the trigger. It was an accident.'

'Go away, go away. I don't want to hear this,' Lester protested, becoming more agitated by the minute. His face reddened and before his dinner companions could intervene Lester gripped his chest in pain and fell to the floor, the victim of a heart attack. At the hospital he was revived but given only days to live. With that knowledge and the belief that his dead brother had been urging him to confess before it was too late, he told the story of that fatal shooting to the police who had gathered at his bedside.

KILLING FOR COMPANY

James had been vindicated again. But this was not the end of the story – not yet. The detectives were puzzled as to why the sixth grave was dug outside the circle formed by the others. Then it occurred to them – this one marked the beginning of a second circle. The killer was still out there and on the prowl for new victims.

Eddie had been accidentally shot by Lester Petrocelli, but someone was kidnapping boys of roughly the same age and burying them alive at the spot where Eddie had died. Could it be that the killer did not have the heart for cold-blooded murder, but was insane – perhaps driven by grief to kill to keep Eddie company?

While the police were considering this possibility James begged the dead boys to appear before him one last time and reveal the name of the killer.

As their spirits gathered in the darkness James sank into a light trance, reliving the last abduction – a victim who was still alive and being held in a locked basement until his abductor was ready to bury him by Eddie's side. Now convinced that James' insights could be acted upon, the lead detective ordered her team back to the nature reserve to save the new boy from certain death, but there was nothing to be seen. While the police officers made snide remarks at the detective's expense James realized his mistake. The killer would not bury the latest victim at Turtleback Reserve as the bodies had all been removed for burial elsewhere. The boy would be buried alive at the cemetery where Eddie was now interred.

Racing through the night, the police reached the cemetery just as a car sped past them through the gate. James jumped out and rushed to the freshly dug grave while the detective turned her car around to give chase. With only seconds to spare James clawed at the ground and rescued the terrified child; at the same moment the detective pulled up outside a house not far away and followed the driver inside. With her gun drawn she moved through the house but the driver was nowhere to be found. Then she noticed the door to the basement. Cautiously she pushed it ajar and descended the steps to a green door – the very same door James saw in his last vision of the abducted boy. There, on her knees scrubbing the cell where her last victim had been held was Molly Katz, mother of Eddie, oblivious to the presence of the policewoman, muttering in her madness how much trouble the little boy had been to keep and to feed.

FORGIVENESS

During her interrogation it transpired that Molly Katz had learnt of her son's death from Richard Petrocelli, who had confessed to covering up the crime as part of his penance on the insistence of his priest. In the madness of her grief she had abducted boys in the belief that they would keep her Eddie company and had no sense of the suffering she had caused them or their families. As the police watched through the one-way mirror of the interrogation room James approached Molly and asked the boys to appear one last time and forgive her, freeing themselves in the process.

CHAPTER FIVE

HIGHWAYS TO HELL

Long, tedious journeys can be hell – particularly if they take a detour through the 'Twilight Zone' where phantom hitch-hikers wait by the side of the road to catch a lift from unwary drivers. Most tales of phantom passengers are no more than urban legends, but those described in the following pages have a ring of authenticity. But if these tales are true they pose the question – if the dead can walk through solid walls, why do some choose to thumb a ride?

ROUTE 666

As every God-fearing Bible reader and horror movie addict knows, '666' is the number of the beast – the Anti-Christ – who is prophesied to arise at the end of days for the final apocalyptic battle between good and evil. So what possessed an American highway official to name the western branch of the Chicago to Los Angeles highway US

666 is anyone's guess. Clearly he wasn't superstitious, or maybe it didn't occur to him that he might be invoking dark and destructive forces on what was to become known as the 'Devil's Highway'.

The name was well deserved, for few stretches of road could boast such a catalogue of eerie encounters. These ranged from phantom hitch-hikers to blazing trucks that would bear down behind a lone driver at high speed, forcing him to put the pedal to the floor or risk being incinerated or driven off the road. There were also tales of savage dogs which would give chase, clawing and biting at tyres until the driver could outpace them. But wild dogs wouldn't attack a speeding car so these too would be attributed to supernatural beasts. It's possible that drivers were confusing these hounds from hell with a particular breed of shape-shifter known in the South-west as skinwalkers, which were believed to assume the form of a man or animal then vanish the moment they had forced a driver to swerve into the oncoming traffic. There were numerous stories of gaunt, cadaverous figures materializing on the back seats of vehicles and scaring the living daylights out of unsuspecting drivers who caught a glimpse of their phantom passengers in their rear-view mirrors. More than a few drivers have stumbled from the wreckage ranting about the stranger on the back seat only for the cops to blame it on drink, drugs or fatigue. Some crash site investigators have even attributed the unusually high incidence of accidents on the route during the 1970s to a form of mass hysteria created by public interest in all things demonic during the decade which spawned a host of diabolical movies including *The Exorcist*, *The Omen* and not forgetting the possessed truck of Steven Spielberg's *Duel*.

Of course, maybe it really was Hell and not Hollywood which was casting its shadow over this godforsaken highway. By 1991 the road's reputation was so bad that parts of it were practically deserted.

Drivers would make tortuously long detours rather than risk falling prey to the many apparitions that were said to haunt it, though many were simply put off by the prospect of breaking down in the Arizona desert or driving over the edge of the twisting mountain passes. It didn't help that souvenir hunters were repeatedly stealing the road signs, leaving tourists scratching their heads as to which turning to take. Highway officials were also receiving complaints from truck stops and filling stations, complaining that trade was practically non-existent and demanding a name change. It was probably this commercial consideration rather than any talk of a curse that finally persuaded the Joint Board of Interstate Highways to redesignate it US 191. Since then the number of inexplicable incidents has decreased dramatically, but even today only the most trusting drivers will pull over for hitch-hikers and even these make sure they stay wide awake and alert at all times.

THE DEAD ZONE

If you're planning to visit Florida in the near future, take a tip from the locals and avoid travelling on Interstate 4 just north of Orlando, especially the 400-metre stretch south of the St John's River Bridge. It's not the daily gridlock that could ruin your vacation, but something intangible and unnerving which is said to account for the uncommonly high accident rate at that spot. Mobile phones and car radios are plagued with static, or even worse, they pick up disturbing, ethereal voices which led to the locals naming this spot the 'Dead Zone'.

There is a sound historical basis for the name; back in 1885 the last surviving members of a devout Roman Catholic community known as St Joseph's Colony died of yellow fever, and were unceremoniously disposed of by other settlers in a field that served as the cemetery.

Contrary to their dying wish, they were denied the benefit of a Christian burial as there was no priest to officiate at the ceremony. The farmer who worked that land avoided the graves and was spared any supernatural activity, but when the construction workers arrived to build the highway in 1960 they didn't bother to disinter and rebury the bodies. They simply levelled the plot and began to concrete it over. And that's when the troubles began.

While the surface was being laid, Hurricane Donna cut a swathe through Florida, causing unprecedented destruction which set the project back several months. Witnesses claim that the epicentre of the storm appeared to be plumb centre in the 'Field of the Dead' where the graves had been. Since then there have been sightings of so-called 'ghost lights' at night which tired drivers have swerved to avoid, mistaking them for approaching headlights, and then there are the ominous dark clouds which appear in bright daylight and whisk across the lanes, causing speeding drivers to slam on the brakes, afraid that they might be ploughing into a flock of birds or a stray animal. No one knows how many accidents have been caused by these manifestations and we are never likely to know how many fatalities can be attributed to them as those who can tell us have joined the unquiet spirits in the Dead Zone.

THE HAUNTED HIGHWAY

Another stretch of highway to avoid is the Pine Barrens section of the Garden State Parkway, which appears to offer a comparatively quiet back road out of New Jersey. Many unsuspecting motorists have lived to regret taking this scenic route through the fog-wreathed forests outside Delaware – especially those who chose to drive at night. Phantom hitch-hikers are a staple ingredient of urban legend, but the 'Parkway Phantom' is no myth. He's the real deal.

The New Jersey state police have been forced to file several reports by terrified drivers who claim to have swerved to avoid a tall thin man in shabby clothes who has been seen running on to the northbound lanes near exit 82 waving his arms frantically as if trying to flag down the speeding cars. A number of accidents have been blamed on his sudden appearance in the middle of a road which is otherwise straight and safe. Sightings of a stranded motorist answering the same description have been recorded elsewhere along the route. This lean figure, dressed in an old-fashioned long coat, is frequently seen standing beside a wrecked car at the side of the road attempting to wave down passing traffic. But whenever someone pulls over to offer help they find both the driver and the vehicle have disappeared.

PHANTOM HITCH-HIKERS

Phantom hitch-hikers are a common urban legend in places as far apart as Malaysia, Hawaii and Russia. Most are dismissed out of hand as mere folk tales, but there are some which are worth closer investigation.

In the 1950s an American couple and their friend were driving to a dance when they stopped to offer a lift to a young blonde girl who was standing at the side of the road. It was a cold evening but she was wearing only a thin white dress and after climbing into the back of the car she commented on how warm it was. She told them her name was Rose White and during the course of conversation accepted their invitation to join them at the dance.

The evening was a success, but both men noted that their new friend was cold to the touch when they took turns dancing with her. Afterwards they dropped her off at the spot by the roadside where they had met and subsequently arranged to meet again the next day at an address she gave them.

But when they arrived there the following day they were shocked to find themselves outside a convent. When they told their story to one of the nuns she produced a photo of Rose which they immediately identified as the girl they had given the lift to. Then the nun took them outside to the cemetery and showed them Rose's grave. She explained that they were not the first people to come looking for Rose White. Every fifteen years, on the anniversary of her death, she would appear at the roadside in the hope of finding the company she longed for from the cold solitude of the grave.

A similar story is told in France of two married couples who picked up a young female hitch-hiker en route to Montpellier in 1981. The girl sat between the two women on the back seat and said nothing for the entire length of the journey. Then suddenly she screamed, causing the driver to brake. But there was nothing in the road. Then the two wives screamed and the men looked back to see the girl had gone – vanished into thin air.

Such stories, corroborated by several witnesses, appear to be genuine incidents of paranormal activity, but there is a more mundane explanation offered for those incidents in which a lone driver gives a lift to a hitch-hiker who promptly disappears without saying so much as 'goodbye'. Doctors have a term for this form of hallucination. They call it hypoxia and claim it is caused by a lack of oxygen to the brain often incurred during long car journeys, specifically when the driver has been smoking.

The most famous case of a phantom hitch-hiker was that experienced by South African army corporal Dawie van Jaarsveld. In 1978 Jaarsveld was riding his motorbike to meet his girlfriend in Uniondale, Cape Province when he saw a dark-haired young girl waiting by the side of the road. She accepted his offer of a lift into town and put on the spare helmet he kept for passengers. A few

It was a cold evening but she was wearing only a thin white dress.

miles further on he pulled over because the bike was behaving oddly, only to discover that his passenger had gone. But the thing which unnerved him was seeing that the spare helmet was still strapped to the bike. Had he imagined the whole episode, or was it possible that the experience had occurred, but in some other reality? Crazy though it might sound, the latter seems more likely as Jaarsveld was later able to positively identify the girl from a photograph which he would not have done had he imagined the whole incident. She was 22-year-old Maria Roux, who had been killed in a car crash in April 1968 on the same stretch of road.

THE BLONDE OF BLUEBELL HILL

Pranksters, drunk drivers and attention-seekers are frequently found to have been the source of many phantom hitch-hiker stories, but those who have reported running over a young female ghost at the notorious accident black spot Bluebell Hill in the English county of Kent appear to have been in deadly earnest.

In 1972 a driver by the unusual name of Mr Goodenough went to the local police to report knocking down a young girl whose body he had covered with a blanket. But when the police arrived at the scene the body was gone.

There was no sign of blood, only the blanket and the skid marks where the 'accident' was said to have happened. Twenty years later the same thing happened again. A driver by the name of Mr Sharpe rushed into the local police station to report killing a young girl who had run out in front of his car before he had time to brake. Again, when the police drove out to the scene there was no body to be found. Curiously, both drivers had described the same girl – a young blonde wearing a white dress.

CHAPTER SIX

HAUNTED HOMES

If you thought that ghosts only haunt crumbling castles and historic houses, think again. Today's spectral squatters are more likely to take up residence in a suburban semi where they can make a real nuisance of themselves. And if it's your home that's haunted, don't blame your uninvited guests – they may just have taken exception to your chosen colour scheme or even your taste in music. So prepare to consult a Ouija board the next time you're considering a makeover.

'For who can wonder that man should feel a vague belief in tales of disembodied spirits wandering through those places which they once dearly affected, when he himself, scarcely less separated from his old world than they, is for ever lingering upon past emotions and bygone times, and hovering, the ghost of his former self, about the places and people that warmed his heart of old?'

CHARLES DICKENS, *Master Humphrey's Clock*

IN EVERY DREAM HOME A HEARTACHE

'. . . if our ancestors attached too much importance
to these ill-understood arcana of the night side
of nature, we have attached too little.'

CATHERINE CROWE, *The Night Side of Nature*, 1848

The days when ghosts swept through cobwebbed corridors rattling rusty chains are long gone. Today's restless spirits are more likely to karaoke with MTV if they don't get the respect and recognition they believe they deserve. At least that's the message delivered by the late Professor Broersma, who died just before Christmas 1987 in the house he built at 2115 Martingale Drive in a suburb of Oklahoma City. A house which he later returned to haunt until the new owners wised up to what he wanted.

The professor evidently found it difficult to communicate at first, if the experiences of the new owners were anything to go by. In fact there were several new residents of the house in quick succession, each driven out by inexplicable noises and occurrences until, in 1994, newlyweds Jon and Agi Lurtz moved in. Jon and Agi were not put off by tales of a restless spirit or the fact that one previous owner had reportedly fled, leaving all his earthly possessions behind. The house was all that they had dreamed of and they were not going to be evicted by anyone, living or dead.

The professor's campaign of intimidation began with regular radio broadcasts in the middle of the night – and they were loud, very loud. Try as they might, the couple couldn't locate the source of the signal.

Their own radio was unplugged. What's more, it was not a station they recognized. It was broadcasting old news from years gone by. It was like living through an episode of *The Twilight Zone*.

Eventually, they came to the conclusion that the sound was coming from beneath the floorboards. But when they lifted them, there was no radio to be found.

Having failed to dislodge the couple, the ghost tried a new tactic. He took possession of the hi-fi and began blasting out heavy metal music at ear-bleeding volumes. His favourite band apparently was the German techno-grunge group Rammstein, whose aural assault of overdriven guitars threatened to bring down plaster from the ceiling. Jon and Agi would frequently return from a shopping trip to find the hi-fi going at full blast, but the equipment had always been switched off before they had left the house.

But the professor had reckoned without Agi, a practical and determined young woman who had lived in haunted houses before and learnt how to assert her rights when confronted with spectral squatters.

One night in 1998 she awoke to see the figure of a man standing at the foot of her bed and, assuming it to be the professor, she demanded to know what he wanted. In a foreign accent he replied that all he wanted was an obituary as he had never had one. And with that he faded away.

All things considered, it didn't seem an unreasonable request and so later that day Agi began to research into the professor's past.

She discovered that his grievances were well founded. His death had not been reported in the local paper and no acknowledgement of his considerable achievements had been made. During the Second World War the Dutch-born academic had served with distinction in the resistance movement at considerable risk to himself, after which he moved to America. There he contributed to the development of advanced sensor technology for NASA (National Aeronautics and Space Administration). All of these accomplishments were listed in Agi's glowing obituary which she wrote for the local paper. They were also included in the eulogy she read aloud at a belated memorial service that she arranged to commemorate his life. It was all the brooding spirit wanted, for immediately afterwards the disturbances ceased.

Some people prefer to keep their achievements to themselves, but clearly the professor felt that he was overdue some recognition before he could rest in peace.

'I guess he felt that he deserved that,' Agi told the paper. 'He needed that before he could go on.'

HOUSE BY THE CEMETERY

In Stephen Spielberg's horror movie *Poltergeist*, a suburban family find themselves in the midst of a storm of paranormal activity which has been stirred up by restless spirits furious at the developers who desecrated their graves. Of course, such things don't happen in real life – or do they?

In 1983 Ben and Jean Williams learnt that such terrifying experiences can and do happen to ordinary people if they are unlucky enough to buy a home built on the site of a former burial ground.

When the couple first moved into their dream home they were delighted both with the house and the location. The new development at Newport, Texas was within commuting distance of Houston and boasted immaculate landscaped gardens and highly desirable upmarket homes. But there was a catch. Their garden seemed to attract an unusual number of poisonous snakes. But this was not all. Lights would switch themselves on and off, the garage door repeatedly malfunctioned and the atmosphere felt unusually oppressive. No matter how often they told themselves that they were now living the life they had always dreamed of, they could not shake off a sense of foreboding or the feeling that something, or someone, was watching them.

Whenever something inexplicable occurred, they came up with a rational explanation. The lights and garage door could be due to faulty wiring, the snakes to some natural phenomenon that would be unearthed one day and their paranoia to the stress of moving.

But there was no explanation for the series of large rectangular holes which seemed to form a pattern in their lawn. As soon as they filled them in, the soil would drain out of them, leaving the same grave-shaped impressions. It was the talk of the neighbourhood. Their unspoken suspicions finally surfaced when contractors began excavating the back yard of the home belonging to their neighbours Sam and Judith Haney and unearthed a pair of rotting coffins containing the corpses of a man and a woman. Nobody slept soundly on the Newport development that night.

The following day, their curiosity aroused, the Newport neighbours banded together to make not-so-discreet inquiries into the history of the site and discovered that it had once been the last resting place of poor black citizens of that region, many of them former slaves.

They even managed to locate a retired black gravedigger who was able to identify the disinterred remains as those of Bettie and Charlie Thomas, who had died during the Depression. Out of genuine respect for the deceased, the Haneys insisted that the bodies be reburied in the garden and given a decent Christian funeral service. But that did not appear to have appeased the dead couple, or to pacify the sixty or so former occupants of Newport's Black Hope Cemetery. Over the following days the Haneys were subjected to a barrage of poltergeist activity: a clock spat sparks, phantom footsteps marched up and down the empty rooms after dark and a pair of Judith's shoes disappeared, only to turn up on Bettie's freshly dug grave. That was it for the Haneys. They instigated legal action against the developer and won the case, but it was overturned on appeal, so they took the only course of action left open to them. They packed up and moved out, leaving a perfectly good house to the ghosts.

Meanwhile, Ben and Jean Williams were seriously considering selling up and moving out, but rumours of the weird goings-on had spread through the real estate community and no one was interested in having the house on their books. Then one night Ben returned home late to see a figure standing at the end of his bed while his wife slept. It was the last straw. They decided that if they were to succeed where their neighbours had failed in suing the developer they would have to provide physical proof. So, in the belief that other bodies were buried in their back garden they decided to unearth these themselves. Jean began digging one afternoon but found the task too tiring so she gave the spade to her 30-year-old daughter, Tina. After only a short while Tina complained of breathlessness and chest pains, then collapsed. She died two days later. The Williams family moved out shortly afterwards and settled in Montana.

THE SPECTRAL SQUATTER

There's only one thing worse than living with a ghost and that's living with a ghost with attitude. Housewife Frances Freeborn found this out to her cost when she moved into her new home in Bakersfield, California in November 1981.

Apparently, the previous owner, Meg Lyons, had departed the property and this earthly life in a hurry, leaving not only her furniture behind but also her clothes which were still hanging in the wardrobe. Frances wasted no time in disposing of everything in preparation for redecorating, but Ms Lyons' spirit was evidently not ready to depart in peace.

The first sign that something was not quite right came with a series of loud noises in the kitchen which Frances attributed to faulty plumbing. But the local handyman could find nothing wrong with the pipes or the heating system. As soon as he had packed up his tools the banging resumed. Frances shrugged it off as one of those things that can't be explained, but in the following days she started to doubt her own sanity when the kitchen cupboards opened by themselves and the lights that she had switched off turned themselves back on again whenever she went out.

Although she was not by nature a nervous woman, she began to feel decidedly uneasy as the weeks went by. Instead of enjoying putting her own personal touches to the house she began to get the distinct impression that someone else was looking over her shoulder and that they disapproved of the changes she was making. A framed antique photograph that she tried to hang was repeatedly taken down undamaged and left propped up against the skirting while Frances was occupied elsewhere. This occurred no fewer than five times, leaving an increasingly uneasy Frances in no doubt that she would have to find another spot for the photo. Not long afterwards the late Ms Lyons' son-in-law came to call and was not surprised to learn of the moving picture. His mother-in-law had hung a similar photo in that very spot and was clearly not happy with its replacement.

Frances stuck it out through the New Year but come spring even the blossoming trees and flowers in the garden couldn't raise her spirits. She made one last determined effort to cheer up the old place and impose her personality upon it. She spent a small fortune at the local DIY store and returned home to smarten up the master bedroom. But the very next morning during breakfast while she looked through colour charts the windows and doors flew open, then slammed closed again as if unseen hands were showing her the nearest exit. Frances took the hint. Still dressed in her nightgown, she snatched up her barking dog and headed for the front door. But something was blocking her retreat.

'There was a zone of pressure, a mass out in the hall,' she later said, 'as if something ominous and ugly was concentrated there. I realized I had to get out of the house or I would die.'

With an enormous effort she screamed at the top of her voice and braced herself against the malevolent mass as if tearing through a downpour. A moment later she was out of the door, sprinting down the path to her car. She never looked back.

A LEGAL MATTER

In a similar case, the new owners of a large Victorian-style house in upstate New York took the seller to court in an attempt to recover their deposit on the grounds that they hadn't been informed that the house was haunted. The previous owner, Helen Ackley, responded by saying that the house's reputation for ghostly goings-on was common knowledge. She had, in fact, published several accounts of her experiences, as a result of which her home had been included in a walking tour of supernatural sites. But she had been less candid with potential purchasers, if the buyers Jeffrey and Patrice Stambovsky were to be believed. 'We were victims of ectoplasmic fraud,' the irate Jeffrey complained to reporters covering the case. The press relished the story, but the New York Appellate Court considered the matter seriously and ruled that, even if the ghostly guests did not actually exist, it was sufficient that some future buyer might believe in them and be dissuaded from purchasing the house as a result. Judge Justice Rubin summed up the decision by saying:

'*Applying the strict rule of* caveat emptor (*buyer beware*) *to a contract involving a house possessed by poltergeists conjures up visions of a psychic or medium routinely accompanying the structural engineers and Terminix man on an inspection of every home subject to a contract of sale.*

'*In the interest of avoiding such untenable consequences, the notion that a haunting is a condition which can and should be ascertained upon reasonable inspection of the premises is a hobgoblin, which should be exorcized from the body of legal precedent and quietly laid to rest.*'

PHANTOM PHOTOS

Little Lisa Swift hated piano lessons. It wasn't that she had no patience for practising. It was the accompanist she objected to – a 7,000-year-old Native American who played a discordant and distinctly haunting tune on his wooden flute whenever she sat down to play. And then there were the shadows which seemed to follow her from room to room, accompanied by the sweet scent of burning wood. But none of these unsettling scents or sounds bothered her mother, California housewife Rita Swift, until much later. In the summer of 1969 Rita was too preoccupied with her new hobby, taking photographs of the family home and the pet cat. There was nothing remarkable about the camera she was using back then. It was an old Kodak Brownie Hawkeye and the film was standard black and white stock. So maybe it was something in the quality of the light in the backyard that September, or maybe there was a fault in the film or the camera because there was no rational explanation for the images which appeared on the last three frames when the negatives were developed thirty years later.

Of course, it might have been the delay in processing the film which created the ghostly apparitions. Fogging is a common fault in amateur photography caused by light leaking into the camera casing and these milky white streaks have been mistaken for ghosts in the past. But the prints Rita Swift collected from the photo shop in 1999 were pin sharp and the strangers she had unknowingly photographed all those years ago were certainly not her neighbours.

The first shot showed three Native Americans in traditional costume dancing in a line. The other two captured a tribe in ceremonial dress grouped around a row of bodies prepared for ritual cremation.

The thought occurred to Rita that someone at the photo store must have been playing a prank, but the other images on the roll were all of her own family. It couldn't have been tampered with by anyone in the family as she had locked the camera with the film still inside it in a trunk in September 1969 and no one had touched it until she found it by accident thirty years later.

If the Swift home had been built on a Native American burial ground it would explain many things.

When she plucked up the courage to show the photos to Native Americans living nearby they refused to look at them more closely, for fear of intruding on a sacred ceremony.

If the Swift home had been built on a Native American burial ground it would explain the ghostly flute and the smell of burning wood, but without physical evidence cynics would say that it was all down to the imagination and that one can see anything in a blurry or faded photograph if one wants to.

But that does not explain the charred bones unearthed in the Swifts' backyard in 1962, seven years before the spooky photos were taken. Fortunately, someone had the presence of mind to send them to the California State College at Long Beach for analysis.

The experts there identified them as the partially cremated remains of a Native American female dating back approximately 7,000 years. It's a pity the Swifts didn't develop the photos earlier. If they had, maybe they wouldn't have built an extension on the site or placed the piano where the cremation took place. Little Lisa Swift might have been a more accomplished pianist if they had.

THE FACE IN THE WINDOW

'Everything that relates, whether closely or more distantly, to psychic phenomena and to the action of psychic forces in general, should be studied just like any other science. There is nothing miraculous or supernatural in them, nothing that should engender or keep alive superstition.'
ALEXANDRA DAVID-NEEL, *Magic and Mystery in Tibet*, 1932

Even in the days before digital photography, photographs were comparatively easy to fake. Convincing apparitions could be created both deliberately and accidentally through double exposure and tricks of the light such as lens flare. But by the 1990s no self-respecting news editor would be taken in by such primitive tricks, so when *Indianapolis Star* photographer Mike Fender printed what appeared to be a genuine spook shot he thought long and hard about whether he should submit it and risk losing his job or destroy it.

On the morning of 29 April 1997 Fender had been assigned to record the removal of a historic 19th-century, Gothic Revival-style farmhouse from a hilltop just outside town to a choice location where it could be preserved by the Historic Landmarks Foundation. It was a delicate operation for the hauliers who had to manhandle the fragile 24-room home without dismantling it, but it should have been a routine assignment for Fender. Being a methodical and conscientious employee he took several shots from every conceivable angle. Then as he stood in front of the trailer on which the house had been secured for its short journey, he noticed what he thought was a little girl in a blue dress standing at an upstairs window looking apprehensively at the scene below. But that couldn't be. The house was empty. It must have been the light playing on the curtains.

The next day the story appeared alongside the photo. Fender had had a deadline to meet and he had taken the chance that no one would notice the tiny figure in the window. But he was wrong.

'We got hundreds of calls,' he was later to say. 'Things like this usually fade after a day or two, but this went on and on and on.'

Everyone, it seemed, had a theory. It was the restless spirit of a little girl who had fallen to her death from the balcony; she had been a murder victim or she had been awoken from her eternal rest by the disturbance to her former home. But research by the Historic Landmarks Foundation had failed to unearth any records that would support any of these theories and the numerous inquiries which followed.

Fender, anxious to disassociate himself from anything 'kookie', subjected the picture to digital analysis. He scanned it into his computer and enlarged it in the expectation that the illusion would dissolve. But to his puzzlement it remained clearly an image of a little girl in a blue dress. Only there was one element of the picture that no one had noticed until it was enlarged. The little girl had no face.

THE FACE IN THE FLAMES

One of the most startling and controversial phantoms on film is that captured by an English amateur photographer, Tony O'Rahilly, during a blaze at Wem Town Hall, Shropshire in November 1995. O'Rahilly hadn't noticed anything unusual at the time, but when he developed the film there was no mistaking the image of a young girl standing in an open doorway on the fire escape. Two professional photographers (Tony Adams of the *Shropshire Star* and an expert from the *Daily Express*) examined both the print and the negative, after which they declared themselves satisfied that it was not a hoax. The latter concluded that a hoaxer would have made a better job of it (though later research would prove otherwise).

It was then passed to the former president of the Royal Photographic Society, Dr Vernon Harrison, then a member of the Association for the Scientific Study of Anomalous Phenomena (ASSAP), who stated that he was confident the photograph was genuine. However, Dr Harrison was puzzled by the fact that the head of the girl appeared to be above the railings of the fire escape while her body, if that's what it was, seemed to be behind them. Also a belt around her waist looked as if it extended in a line across and beyond her body instead of being wrapped around her. The image hadn't been faked, Dr Harrison concluded, but it was possible that the image was an illusion created by falling debris and tricks of the light. Subsequent examination of the fire service video of the blaze revealed a blackened roof beam where the girl's 'belt' had been, but it did not account for the unmistakable image of her 'face'.

The BBC (British Broadcasting Corporation) was next in line to examine the photo and submitted it to the experts of the National Photographic Museum as part of an investigation for their *Out Of This World* programme. The boffins at the museum pointed out several horizontal lines across the girl's face which they concluded indicated that it had been computer generated, but Phil Walton of the ASSAP responded that 'it seemed the BBC had already made up their mind that

The head of the girl appeared to be above the railings, while her body seemed to be behind them.

the photograph was a hoax . . . I've a suspicion that the scan lines were incurred during the process they had used to produce the enlargement.'

Looking closely at the photograph, it is hard to imagine that the image could have been created by smoke and falling debris snapped at just the right moment when it happened to form a clearly discernible face.

SPOOKS AT PSYCHIC SCHOOL

Burning embers do not, however, explain away the luminous swirls of vapour which have appeared on numerous photos taken by various visitors over the years to Stansted Hall, centre of the National Spiritualist Union. Perhaps it's not surprising that Stansted should be such a hive of paranormal activity as the hall is the venue for Britain's 'psychic school', where experienced psychics offer training courses and practical demonstrations of mediumship. But the ghostly manifestations might not be phantoms of former pupils, but are more likely to be the accumulation of residual personal energy generated by the fledgling mediums who attend the lectures and courses.

CANDID CAMERA

Of course, it would be more convincing if such images were caught on video and that is exactly what occurred early on an October morning in 1991 in a nightclub in Lancashire, northern England. At 4.32am the burglar alarm at the club was triggered by the appearance of a phantom figure which was evidently sufficiently solid to be picked up by its sensors.

When the manager arrived he ordered the night staff to search the building, but no signs of a break-in were found and all the employees could account for their whereabouts at the time. Baffled as to what might have activated the alarm, the manager ordered the surveillance tapes to be played. There for all to see was a ghostly figure moving soundlessly through the corridor and then passing through a solid locked door to the cash office. No explanation has been offered to explain the phenomenon.

THE SPIRIT OF ROOM 422

*'There are many ways of opening the doors of perception.
Not all of them enable you to control what comes
through the open doors, or to get them shut again.'*

GUY LYON PLAYFAIR, *The Indefinite Boundary*, 1976

When best-selling horror author Stephen King wrote *The Shining*, about a haunted hotel which exerts an evil influence on its occupants, he may have taken inspiration from a real-life hostelry – the Holiday Inn, Grand Island in Buffalo, New York.

Although this impressive establishment doesn't boast the remote mountainous setting of its fictional counterpart, it promises guests an equally memorable stay.

Many have commented on hearing what sounds like a child running along the empty halls and girlish giggling echoing in room 422. Staff have reported hearing a child calling their names and have had their duties interrupted by mischievous antics so often that they have come to refer to it affectionately as Tanya.

Locals say that she is the ghost of a child who burned to death in a fire in the house that occupied the site on which the hotel was built, but if that is true, she does not appear to be a troubled spirit. Apparently Tanya enjoys doing the same things all little girls like doing at her age, including bouncing on newly made beds and hiding cleaning products from the chambermaids. But in case anyone should suggest that it's just a clever marketing gimmick to drum up business for those who enjoy a good scare, staff are quick to point out that Tanya has been caught on camera, in the form of ghost lights which can be seen floating eerily down the corridors.

Curiously, this is one restless spirit that people don't seem to fear. In fact, they actually welcome it. Many a guest has been known to voice their disappointment if they arrive to find that room 422 is occupied, a problem some avoid by booking months in advance.

HAUNTED HOTELS

The palatial, palm-lined Renaissance Vinoy Hotel in St Petersburg, Florida was built in the 'Roaring Twenties' for film stars, playboys and

Does a shadowy figure haunt the Renaissance Vinoy Hotel which was built during the 'Roaring Twenties' in St Petersburg, Florida?

sporting celebrities, but now it seems it is home to some uninvited and rather unruly guests. In an interview for *Haunted Baseball*, relief pitcher Scott Williamson of Tampa Bay's local team, the Devil Rays, told author Dan Gordon of the night he agreed to play host to a visiting team staying at the Vinoy in June 2003.

After climbing into bed and turning out the lights, Williamson glanced through the parted curtains and thought he saw a faint luminous glow near the pool. At the sight of this a tingling sensation electrified his entire body as if someone were watching him. It unnerved him, but he tried to shrug it off and get some sleep. Rolling over on to his front, he suddenly felt pressure as if someone was pushing down on him, which gave him trouble breathing. With an effort, he turned over on to his back, but it still felt as if someone were sitting on him. When he opened his eyes he saw a shadowy figure standing by the window. It was a man dressed in a long coat that seemed to belong to the 1930s or 1940s. Then it was gone.

Williamson was so distressed that he immediately phoned his wife, who worked in a nearby hospital, and asked her if there was any medical reason that might explain the pressure on his chest. He was relieved to hear that there was unlikely to be anything physically wrong as he had no other symptoms, but the feeling of unease wouldn't leave him.

The next day, after a restless night's sleep, he asked a friend to research the history of the hotel and find out if there was a basis for the phantom presence. Indeed, there was. The previous owner of the property, who had lived in the house before it had been converted into a hotel, had died there after a fire. His name, incredibly, was also Williamson.

It wasn't the last sighting of the shadowy stranger at the Vinoy.

The very next day, at 5am, pitcher Frank Velasquez of the Pittsburgh Pirates awoke to see a transparent figure standing by the desk at the window. Velasquez later described him as being a sandy-haired and blue-eyed man wearing a long-sleeved white shirt and khaki-coloured trousers. Both his manner of dress and his haircut gave the pitcher the distinct impression that the visitor came from a previous age.

To make sure he was not dreaming, Velasquez closed his eyes for a moment then opened them again. Sure enough, the man was still standing there. But being travel-weary, Velasquez just turned over and went back to sleep. It was only later that he learned of Williamson's story, which he felt confirmed his own experience.

'The fact that it lined up with someone's story that I never knew anything about just kind of helps me know that it was real.'

But apparently that wasn't the only sighting of the 'old gentleman' that night. The team's assistant was standing in the hall trying to fiddle his room key into the lock when a man in a tailored suit passed soundlessly by, looking like an extra from a Humphrey Bogart movie. Unable to open the door, the assistant turned to ask the old man for help but the corridor was empty.

When these stories began to circulate among the players several elected to move out, while others chose to commute from their home to the ballpark and back every day rather than have to sleep overnight in the hotel. The wife of one player fled with her children in the middle of the night when the taps in their bathroom repeatedly turned themselves on and there were numerous stories of flickering lights, slamming doors, clothes that mysteriously moved from the wardrobe to the bed and electrical cables which inexplicably pulled themselves out of the wall sockets and wrapped themselves around appliances.

But without doubt the most unsettling story was that told by Devil Ray pitcher Jon Switzer and his wife, who were awoken one night in their room on the fifth floor by the sound of scratching coming from the wall behind the headboard. They assumed it was a rat, but after a few moments it stopped and they went back to sleep. A quarter of an hour later it began again, but this time it was so loud that the Switzers leapt out of bed and turned on the lights.

To their horror and utter astonishment, they saw what appeared to be the painting above their bed come to life. It was a simple garden scene depicting a Victorian lady holding a basket with her right hand and her left resting on her chin. But now her left hand was scratching desperately at the glass as if trying to get out! Switzer and his wife exited the room faster than you could say 'Scooby Doo'.

PHANTOM PITCHERS

Sportsmen are notoriously superstitious and baseball players are known to be more superstitious than most. They covet lucky bats, gloves that caught a curved ball and even shoes in which they made a winning home run. Many have their own pre-game rituals that help to calm their nerves which can involve putting on their equipment in a particular order and refusing to change worn-out shirts in case they interrupt a winning streak, while some even invoke the name of the great stars of the sport who have departed to play in the great stadium in the sky. It's a game steeped in tradition and its own mythology, so it is no surprise that the players have more than their share of ghost stories.

Ask any player to name the most haunted ballpark and they will all name Wrigley Field, home of the Chicago Cubs, where the ashes of Charlie Grimm, the Cubs manager during the 1930s, are said to have been scattered. His ghost has been seen by several security guards patrolling the stadium after dark and he is blamed for the unnerving phone calls to the dugout when the building is empty. Whenever the guards summon the nerve to pick up the receiver all they hear is an eerie silence, but they say that Charlie is on the other end giving orders from the bullpen where he used to direct the game. The bullpen phone is a direct line, so there is no way that anyone could be calling from outside the stadium and the security guards are too spooked to play tricks of that sort on each other.

Wrigley is positively crawling with spirits of players and fans who couldn't let death come between them and their beloved game. Some fans have even had their own ashes scattered secretly at the ground, which might account for the countless balls which disappear into the ivy. At one point, the owners of the ground brought in paranormal researchers to investigate the numerous sightings, but frustratingly their findings were never published.

Dan Gordon, co-author of *Haunted Baseball*, is a mine of lurid tales of hauntings, curses and legends about the game. He told interviewer Jeff Belanger of ghostvillage.com about the strangest legend he unearthed while researching the book.

'Dodger Stadium rests on the land of a former Mexican-American community, Chavez Ravine (and on the site of the former Hebrew Benevolent Society Cemetery, the first Jewish cemetery in LA – behind what is now parking lot 40-41) that was cleared to make room for the ballpark. The stadium rests on the levelled-off crest of a hill overlooking the city and according to urban legend, a couple on their honeymoon taking in a breathtaking view of downtown LA from the hillside (at what is now the southern edge of the stadium parking lot) plummeted from the ravine to their deaths. The story went that the man fell first and upon discovering this, his wife leapt off the ridge. A story handed down from some of the old-time Dodger employees is that every now and then one could see an image of a shrieking woman dressed in white plunging over the cliff.

'A souvenir vendor shared a story with us about his encounter with a "fog-like object" that reminded him of La Llorona stories he'd heard from co-workers. [Author's note: La Llorona is a popular Mexican legend concerning a mother who drowns her own children and is cursed to roam the earth searching for them.] He was working late into the night counting inventory on the top deck behind the left-field seats when he suddenly peered out on to the field and saw the white hazy formation originate at the Dodgers' bullpen and make its way across the field. He would witness the same occurrence happen quite a few times during his twenty years working with the team. He told us, "One time, I actually brought a laser pointer that I used as part of my selling tools in my stand, and I pointed it at it to see what the hell it was, and it didn't disappear. It pretty much hovered around the field."

'He also reported hearing a child following him one evening when he was working on the mezzanine level. We heard reports of phantom footsteps from a lot of stadium workers (particularly the late-night security guards). One security guard told us an eerie story about how he and his fellow officers hear a woman in high heels walking the top deck.

'That's just the tip of the iceberg of stories we discovered about the stadium. We recorded several from merchandise workers who work in the stadium's underground vaults that house historical memorabilia and lead into tunnels that travel deeper into the hill. Add to this the Hopi Legends of the domed headquarters of one of the three lost cities of "Lizard People" alleged to exist further below the stadium and there's a whole lot of behind-the-scenes baseball strangeness in the City of Angels.'

BAD MOJO IN A BUNGALOW – THE SAN PEDRO HAUNTING

'When I see ghosts they look perfectly real and solid – like a living human being. They are not misty; I can't see through them; they don't wear sheets or bloody mummy bandages. They don't have their heads tucked under their arms. They just look like ordinary people, in living color, and sometimes it is hard to tell who is a ghost.'

CHRIS WOODYARD, *Haunted Ohio*

So many amateur ghost-hunters strike out after staking out a promising site for nights on end with nothing to show for their patience but a shot or two of fogged film or a mysterious streak of light which could be caused by lens flare. Barry Conrad and his friends were considerably luckier – if being assaulted by a malevolent entity is what you're after. They bagged the biggest game of the spirit world when they investigated an alleged haunting in a quiet suburb of San Pedro, California and managed to capture much of it on video.

Weldon is a quiet respectable neighbourhood and populated with rows of modest bungalows built at the turn of the previous century (1905). The last place one would expect to find a spook to rival that of *The Amityville Horror*. Fortunately for ghost aficionados, Barry, an experienced TV cameraman, was on hand to record what went on in one particular house during the summer of 1989.

Barry has since produced a video of the investigation and appeared on internet radio 'Paranormal Café' to talk about his nerve-shredding experiences.

'*I was determined to record the phenomena on film to avoid being accused of inventing yet another ghostly "one that got away". But the manifestations began even before I had a chance to unpack my gear. The first time we were in the house I felt pressure as if I was several fathoms underwater. But I really didn't expect to see anything so soon, so I suggested to a professional photographer friend who was with me that he take some photos of the attic where the owner of the house had said she had once seen a disembodied head. There isn't a ladder to the crawl space so my friend had to stand on a milk churn and poke his head through the trapdoor. After taking a few shots he came down and said that he felt someone had been watching him, but that it must just have been because he had heard all the spooky stories about the house. He was laughing it off, but I encouraged him to go back up and take some more shots, this time over his shoulder where he had sensed this presence. He thought it was a waste of time but did it to humour me and a moment later we heard him cry out. He bolted down the stairs and was shaking. All the colour had drained out of his hands. When he had calmed down he told us that just as he was about to squeeze off his third shot something or someone had jerked the camera out of his hands! He'd fled without it and was too frightened to go back and get it. I wouldn't have believed him if I hadn't seen the effect it had had on him. He was a wreck. That's when I knew we were really on to something.*'

While the photographer, Jeff, was catching his breath, Barry went out to the car to get his video recording equipment which included powerful lights and a power supply. When he and Jeff cautiously approached the attic the camera was running, but as soon as Barry poked his head through the opening to film inside the crawl space the fully charged battery was drained of all power and the camera shut off. But the light was working and illuminated the whole loft space. There they could see that the floor was loosely boarded, which would have made a noise if any hoaxer had been hiding up there, and that there was no hiding place for anyone to avoid the glare of their lights. More perplexing was the discovery that the lens had been removed from the camera and left where Jeff thought he had sensed the presence, but the body of the camera had been placed in an open wooden crate on the other side of the loft! As Jeff struggled with shaking hands to screw the lens back on his camera Barry became aware of a 'foul odour' pervading the attic which he later compared to the stench of a rotting corpse. It was time to get out.

As Barry clambered down out of the attic he saw the light on his camera turn green, which meant that power had been restored. Looking up at Jeff, he saw his friend's face contorted in terror. But he clearly couldn't speak. Once they were safely back on the landing Jeff blurted out that he had been too terrified to talk. He had felt a long bony hand pressing into his back. As the friends stood bewildered and trying vainly to take in all that they had experienced they heard the unmistakable sound of footsteps in the empty space above them. According to Barry it sounded like a giant rat scampering across the floorboards. Fortunately, both the sound and the investigator's genuinely horrified reactions were captured on camera.

It took some time before Jeff got his nerve back and agreed to take another peek through the trapdoor. When he did so he saw what he described as a 'black mass' moving from side to side in the half-light. That proved to be the last straw for Jeff, who refused to stay in the house a moment longer. It took all of Barry's persuasive powers to keep him alongside while he recorded an impromptu interview with the owner of the house, Jacqui Hernandez. But that was cut short when all the lights went out.

That night, at Barry's apartment, Jeff awoke screaming that

someone was standing over him and couldn't be consoled. 'It was pretty frightening,' Barry recalled with characteristic understatement. It was to be another month before he had plucked up enough courage to go back to the house for a second look and only then because Jacqui had phoned him in the middle of the night in a highly agitated state and asking for his help. Her exact words were, 'all hell is breaking loose'. Apparently that night she had been in the kitchen when the refrigerator door opened by itself and the cap flew off a bottle of Pepsi, showering her with liquid. She pushed the door closed, but it had opened again. That was when she claimed to have been attacked by an unseen entity which had pinned her to the floor. It took every ounce of her strength and her fear for the safety of her children to break free.

Forty-five minutes later, Barry pulled up in front of the bungalow in time to see Jacqui standing on the front lawn with her baby daughter cradled in one arm and her young son clinging tightly to the other hand.

'She thought we were coming to rescue her,' Barry remembers. 'But we burst out of that van with our cameras and lights like a bunch of Ghostbusters.'

On this occasion Barry had brought reinforcements. Barry and Jeff had stopped off to pick up their friend Gary on the way as he was 'a born sceptic' with a serious interest in the scientific aspect of the paranormal and a person they could count on to look for a rational explanation before he would even consider the possibility of the supernatural.

Inside the house it was suspiciously quiet. But that was soon to change. Gary was keen to explore the attic, having heard about his friends' earlier encounter, and managed to persuade Jeff to accompany him. Barry remained behind in the laundry room underneath the trapdoor nursing his $15,000 video camera, which he was determined to protect after having seen what had happened to Jeff's 35 mm. No sooner had the intrepid pair entered the loft than Barry saw a 'reddish orb' shoot down from the opening and vanish into the wall behind him. Thinking it might have been a flare from a flash he called to the others, but they assured him they hadn't taken any shots. It was then Barry's turn to get that sense that something was watching him from the open door of the bathroom to his right. Then there was the unmistakable sound of a loud groan from the attic and the noise of a struggle. Barry recorded these sounds, which are followed by an eerie pause while he calls out to his friends. But they don't respond. After anxious moments they emerge pale and trembling into the light of the laundry room. Jeff is rubbing his throat, which is marked with deep red weals. In the darkness something had grabbed on to his feet and wrapped a washing line around his neck then strung him up to a nail in the rafters. If Gary hadn't lifted him up and unwound the cord he would have been the first-ever victim of a spectral lynching. In fact, Jeff very nearly didn't make it. While Gary was trying to lift his friend up by the waist to get some slack and loosen the cord, the entity was pulling at Jeff's legs to tighten the noose. At the last moment Gary bent the nail with his bare hands so the cord would come loose. Jeff had blacked out when the noose tightened, but he came to when the cord was loosened and it was then that he had felt something pulling on his legs. Incredible as it must sound the evidence was there on film for all to see in the shape of the angry red welts around Jeff's neck.

'This had started out as spooky fun and games,' Barry remembers, 'but then we realized that it was a seriously dangerous business.'

No one could remember seeing the cord in the loft. On their initial inspection it had been empty apart from the fruit crate and some bric-a-brac. If there had been a cord it was certainly not attached to the nail. What was even more puzzling was the fact that it had been wound around Jeff's neck several times and secured to the nail by a bowline – a seaman's knot. Weldon is a coastal town and it's conceivable that the house had once been owned by a seafaring man. Jacqueline and her children moved out of the house and away from the area after that, but it wasn't quite the end of the haunting. Her friend, Susan Kastenedaz, called in Barry and his ghostbusters to check out her home, which had been built next to a cemetery. It was also a turn-of-the-century home and had been designed by its first owner, John Damon. While Barry was taking exterior shots of the house a side gate flew open by itself, but nothing could be seen with the naked eye. Later when Barry and Susan viewed the footage they could clearly see a light exiting the front door of the house and making a trail across the garden to the gate. As Barry pointed out, there are no fireflies in Southern California and the front of the house was in deep shade when the film was shot. When he tracked the trail through the gate it led into the cemetery and disappeared into the ground over the grave of the late John Damon.

DIARY OF A HAUNTING

Starr and Jessi Chaney, a mother and daughter team of 'certified ghost-hunters' in Nicholasville, Kentucky kept a journal of their experiences in their haunted home beginning in the summer of 2005. These brief extracts, reproduced below, give some idea of what it is like to live with both the fear and fascination of spontaneous paranormal phenomena.

Well, you can just imagine how excited we were to be buying our first home! We closed the loan on the Thursday before Memorial Day. While we were there with the lady who we were buying the house from, she told us that her first husband had passed away in the house several years before. She told us what a loving man he was, so we didn't really think much of it. We figured if he was still hanging around, he'd be following her to her new home with her new husband. We moved in that weekend, and with all the commotion going on with people in and out we didn't notice his presence for several days.

My first experience with George was in our master bathroom. I walked past the open door, and saw a man standing in the bathroom. It took me a moment to realize that my husband wasn't home, so I quickly backtracked . . . only to find, of course, that the figure was gone. My daughters have seen him several times in there as well. He isn't scary, it's just the initial shock that gets ya.

It didn't take long to realize we had another guest in our home, this one a young man. Research hasn't shown any other deaths in our house, so we aren't sure who he is exactly. We can tell you that he likes a good laugh, no doubt. He likes to imitate our voices, so we come running, thinking that another family member is calling us. I can't tell you how many times I've heard 'Mom!' come from the front hallway (where my daughters' bedrooms are), only to go in there and find them asleep or just watching TV and staring at me with a puzzled look at my hurried entrance. Then there are the times when Jessi and Nicki have stuck their head into my office and said, 'What?' Clueless, I say, 'What, what? I didn't say anything.' Never a dull moment!

We aren't quite sure which one of them it is who likes to open the kitchen cabinets though. For nearly a year I went nuts, chastising Jessi and Nicki for leaving them open all the time . . . then one day I was home alone and went into the kitchen to get a drink. Of course, all the cabinet doors were open, so I mumbled under my breath, got my glass and closed them all. After getting my drink, I returned to the office. About an hour later I went into the kitchen to make myself something for lunch, and found all the cabinet doors open again! So, I made a mental note to apologize to my daughters when they got home, fixed my lunch, and left the room.

The most jolting experience I've had was late one night in 2004. I was working on the computer, updating my candle website, and it was close to 3am. It had been a hectic week, and this was the only time I had to get this task done. My husband had long since given up on me coming to bed, and had fallen asleep. I was intent on getting finished, so I barely noticed anything going on around me . . . until I felt a hand on my shoulder. I instantly assumed it was my husband coming to remind me of what time it was, so I quickly said, 'I know it's late, honey, but I really need to get this finished. I'll be to bed in just a b . . .' And that is when I looked over my shoulder and saw no one. At that very time there was a voice from the same area, definitely male; I heard one syllable and then it faded away. I immediately brought out my recorder and began asking questions, but the moment had passed. My visitor no longer had anything to say . . . but boy did he get my heart pumping!

We have gotten some photos with orbs, but nothing extraordinary like a mist or ectoplasm. And even though our fellas love to talk, apparently they don't care for being taped because they have never given us an EVP [electronic voice phenomenon]. Not that we'll quit trying, of course!

Saturday, June 25, 2005 – Nicki had to have her tonsils removed the prior Thursday, so she was in the master bedroom with me and we were watching TV. I had just muted the television, and Nicki was writing me a note (because she still had a hard time speaking). From my office, right next to our bedroom, came the sound of someone knocking on the door (my office door, which I keep closed). We both looked at each other, because it was a definite knock, just like someone knocking on your front door. I got up to see if someone was there, though I couldn't imagine who since we were alone in the house . . . of course, there was no one.

Wednesday, June 29, 2005 – Another incidence of voice mimicry. Nicki came into my office from the den wanting to know what I wanted; I hadn't said anything. We were alone in the house.

Monday, August 1, 2005 – *My birthday! Nicki and I were alone in the house and we heard a clatter from my office. When we went to check it out, 4 of my pillar moulds were on the floor. They had previously been in a box on my shelf. I guess they were saying Happy Birthday, LOL.*

Sunday, August 14, 2005 – *Our whole family was in the den, and we had our 2 dogs (Malachai and Belle) inside with us because it was raining. We were talking back and forth when we all heard a loud voice come from the front of the room that said, 'Puppy!' It didn't sound like a male, so we may have another spirit here now.*

Monday, September 5, 2005 – *We had guests over for the Holiday for a cookout. Shortly after sitting down at the table to eat, we all heard a creaking noise coming from the other side of the kitchen. When we turned to look, one of the cabinet doors was slowly swinging open all on its own.*

Thursday, October 6, 2005 – *Another incidence of voice mimicry. Ed swears he heard me calling out for him while he was in the den. I was in my office working on my computer and hadn't said anything.*

Thursday, October 13, 2005 – *We went out for dinner and upon arriving back home I found several of my incense bundles placed on my desk . . . they were previously on a shelf on the other side of the room.*

Tuesday, October 31, 2005 – *I was alone in the house during the day, working on getting ready for the evening's festivities, when I saw a man walk into our master bathroom. It startled me, to say the least, but I figured Ed must have gotten home early. When I went to the bathroom to check it out, no one was there.*

Sunday, November 27, 2005 – *Jessi, Nicki and I were sitting on the bed in the master bedroom watching a movie when something thumped the bed hard enough to make it shudder. The bed is a queen size waterbed, the floor is carpeted, and underneath the bedroom is solid block concrete.*

Thursday, January 12, 2006 – *Another incidence of voice mimicry. I clearly heard Jessi's voice from our master bathroom, asking me to come* *in there. When I went in I found the room empty. I found Jessi in her bedroom on the other side of the house.*

Wednesday, March 22, 2006 – *While I was alone in the house, I walked into the kitchen to round up some lunch and found all the cabinet doors open. They were closed when I had gone in earlier for breakfast.*

Wednesday, May 17, 2006 – *Nicki's birthday. We noticed the strong scent of Old Spice in the house . . . there isn't even a bottle of the stuff IN our house. My Dad used to wear it on special occasions, so I'm sure he was telling his granddaughter Happy Birthday.*

June through November 2006 – *The activity in the house has really picked up, there is something on nearly a daily basis. Most involve objects being moved from where they were left, our kitchen cabinets being opened and closed, and actual sightings of people in the house. We have seen, several times, someone walk past the 'window' that is above the sink in the kitchen and looks into the den (due to a home extension, the window was removed and there is just a finished open area there now). We hear our cabinets being opened and closed as if someone is looking for something, but upon inspection no one is there.*

August 14, 2007 – *Our ghosts were fairly inactive the first half of the year, we had even begun to think they were no longer around . . . they sure proved us wrong! Jessi, Nicki and I were all in the master bedroom having a girls' night, watching movies and eating popcorn while piled up on the bed, when we heard the back door open. That was followed immediately by footsteps of someone crossing the den and entering the kitchen, and the sound of cabinet doors being opened. We figured Ed had gotten home early, but when Nicki checked it out no one was in the house but us.*

September 13, 2007 – *Today, just as we were setting up for the radio show, Jessi saw what she thought was Ed walking into our bedroom. She said, 'Is Dad home tonight?' to which I replied he wasn't. When we checked the bedroom, of course, we found it empty.*

October 1, 2007 – Things have really started hopping again! For the past week, on a daily basis we have encountered the bathroom and closet doors near the master bedroom opening on their own. We close them, and yank to make sure they are closed. Jessi and I actually happened to be looking down the hall from the master bedroom when the bathroom door opened on the first day it began happening, there was no one or no animal around it. All the other times it has happened we have heard the doors click, as if the handle was being turned, and then hear them open.

Most people would have sold up and moved out when confronted by such inexplicable incidents, but Starr, her husband Ed and their two daughters Jessi and Nicki were fascinated by the phenomenon. They founded an organization called PsyTech to investigate alleged hauntings and offered to organize ghost tours of spooky sites in their native state. Business boomed and the family were so overwhelmed by the response from wannabe ghost-hunters that they decided to offer one-day intensive certificated courses to train people in how to conduct a paranormal investigation.

DEAD FAMOUS

'We are, one and all, so pitifully afraid of the light.'

HENRIK IBSEN, *Ghosts*

LENNON'S GHOST

Rock star Liam Gallagher of Britpop band Oasis reportedly lived in fear of a ghost which haunts his luxury London home.

In a British newspaper interview, a friend of the band confided that Liam had difficulty sleeping because he believed he was being haunted by the phantom of former Beatle John Lennon, who was murdered in

1980. 'He lies awake listening with the lights on. He sometimes wakes up and feels as though he is being watched by someone from another walk of life.'

One would imagine that Liam would welcome the chance to chat with his musical hero, but it seems he feared he was being pursued by the restless spirit. 'I was in Manchester at a mate's house,' Liam confided to a friend after he first encountered Lennon's ghost during an out-of-body experience. 'I turned round and there I was, lying on the bed, and I sort of fell back into my body. There was a presence there and it was him, Lennon.'

Cynics might say that such experiences are often induced by an over-indulgence in alcohol and non-prescription pharmaceuticals, while music critics would no doubt claim that Lennon has come back to claim his share of the royalties for all the tunes the Gallagher brothers ripped off the old Beatles albums.

IN SEARCH OF SINATRA AND OTHER CELEBRITY SPIRITS

Shows with a supernatural theme have become a ratings winner on the small screen in recent years, but sadly for the producers ghosts have proven to be camera-shy, while other paranormal phenomena seldom appear on cue. No matter how talented the programmes' resident psychics might be, they can't guarantee the thrills that viewers demand or even the proof that the scientists and parapsychologists are hoping for.

Take the case of professional psychic Chris Fleming. Chris was co-presenter of the British TV series *Dead Famous*, one of a long line of paranormal reality shows which investigated alleged hauntings and shared their findings with viewers in the safety of their living rooms.

Accompanying Chris on his televised tour was presenter Gail Porter, a self-confessed sceptic in all matters supernatural, who plays Scully to his Mulder. In reality, their investigations offered little more than a few words with the dead celeb's former acquaintances and the staff who now work at the sites of their former haunts. Then it's lights off for a vigil in a darkened room with a video camera and a lot of night-vision shots of the pair looking spooked and talking in awe of 'energy imprints'.

Their first subject was 'ol' Blue Eyes' himself, Frank Sinatra. As they set off on their trip to Las Vegas, Gail contemplated which side of Sinatra would be uncovered – the charming showman or the hard, abrasive friend of the Mob? This was clearly not going to be a serious investigation, but yet another entertainment special with a paranormal theme.

On day one they met with Tony Oppedisano, a 'personal friend' of Sinatra, who shared his impressions of the singer, which amounted to little more than saying that he was a 'very complex man'. It seems that Frank was a believer in reincarnation, which was bad news for 'Mulder and Scully' as it meant that he wouldn't be hanging around his old haunts if he had been reborn. But Tony was certain Frank was watching over him and that his larger-than-life personality guaranteed he would be hanging around the Golden Nugget, the casino and hotel that had been his second home. There, on the fifth floor where Sinatra had his suite, Chris felt 'strong energy', but couldn't identify the source.

In the luxury suite he doused the lights and lit a candle while asking Sinatra to bless them with his presence. Speaking into the camera in the darkness like a resident of the *Big Brother* house, he was reduced to generalities such as 'something just went on' which must have angered ol' Blue Eyes as it was apparently answered by the sound of fingernails scraping on the window, although we couldn't hear it. Or maybe it was just the producer clawing to get out.

STRANGER IN THE NIGHT

On day two, after Chris had shared his 'experiences' in Sinatra's suite the previous night, the pair set off for the Polo Lounge, an exclusive saloon on the banks of Lake Tahoe. En route they stopped in at the Thunderbird Lodge, a playboys' hideaway in the mountains boasting a secret room where Frank played cards with his cronies and allegedly met with the underworld figures who were said to have 'guided' his career. But in spite of all the talk of his larger-than-life personality Frank again failed to put in an appearance, although in the boathouse 'something' drained the batteries in Chris' camera and pushed him as he explored the former owner's bedroom. One has to wonder why a personality as imposing as Sinatra would miss the opportunity of a lifetime to make a comeback on camera.

It almost makes you question your belief in ghosts, or ghost-hunters.

Day three saw our intrepid duo and the camera crew at Calneva, Frank's former residence on the California/Nevada border. It had been built on a sacred Native American tribal ground which might account for the phenomena which have spooked its staff over the years.

During a guided tour Chris and Gail learnt that the staff consider certain areas of the hotel off limits and they saw for themselves the damage to the large picture window in the lounge which mysteriously cracks when no one is looking.

As for the TV which turns itself on in one of the guest cabins, the pair had to take the tour guide's word for that, but there was no doubt in Chris' mind that there was a 'strong imprint' in that particular cabin. Mind you, that was after he had been told this was where Marilyn Monroe had suffered an overdose.

If only the programme's producer or the tour guide had thought to test Chris' abilities by taking him to a cabin where nothing untoward had happened and seeing if he had come up with the same impression after being told that story.

That night, obviously aware that they hadn't come up with anything to justify their travel expenses, or the viewers' patience, Chris took part in a séance in Frank's Celebrity Showroom, a private theatre where Sinatra and his buddies entertained their friends.

Casing the joint before the big event, all Chris could come up with was another of his vague, groan-inducing observations, specifically, 'There's definitely some type of energy up there.'

As parapsychologist and impartial observer Janice Oberding remarked, 'It's very easy to convince yourself that you're feeling something when you get a group like this together,' meaning people who are believers to begin with and who have gathered in expectation of hearing 'something'.

If that's what they wanted, Chris didn't disappoint them. He mumbled that he was feeling 'really cold' and went into a trance during which he claimed he could not only sense Frank's spirit, but could see him 'at the end of a long tunnel'. He also claimed to have been taken over by the spirit of Sammy Davis, Jr, but said nothing in Sammy's voice nor did he imitate his mannerisms, at least not in the clip we were shown.

Then as the performance's climax he channelled the spirit of a Native American, but when asked to 'communicate' by another member of the circle all he could do was produce some incoherent chanting, although once again we can only judge by what was broadcast.

Whether Chris is a genuine psychic is not the question. He may well be the real deal, although he offers no compelling evidence to support this in the programme and too often he seems to bolt at the first sign of a spook. Why invite a clairvoyant to a supposedly haunted location if he is going to leave at the first sign of paranormal activity?

It wasn't as if anything had actually manifested or had thrown objects around. All we had was Chris claiming that he felt 'something' and that he wasn't hanging around to find out what it was! Little old ladies who practise mediumship at Spiritualist churches up and down the country show more backbone.

The Dead Famous team offered nothing substantial to support the belief in life after death other than their vague feelings of being scared of the dark. It's all so inconsequential that if it had been a one-to-one reading with a medium we would feel entitled to our money back. It may have seemed a whizz of an idea in the network executives' meeting, but 'investigations' of this kind give ghost-hunting a bad name.

Quite frankly, it's embarrassing to watch. If you want to see a serious demonstration of spirit communication, you only have to tune in to see the American celebrity psychics John Edward and James Van Praagh in action before a studio audience, or the compelling English 'street psychic' Tony Stockwell and his colleague Colin Fry. All of these presenters offer 'cold' spontaneous and uncannily accurate readings of complete strangers, the details of which are invariably confirmed by their astonished subjects.

The best that can be said for *Dead Famous* is that they haven't made any kind of convincing case for the existence of spooks and spirits – only for the public's seemingly insatiable appetite for celebrities and the supernatural.

PARANORMAL INVESTIGATIONS INC – INTERVIEW WITH LOYD AUERBACH

Loyd Auerbach is director of the Office of Paranormal Investigations and the author of several seminal studies of the subject including *A Paranormal Casebook: Ghost Hunting in the New Millennium* (Atriad Press, 2005), *Ghost Hunting: How to Investigate the Paranormal* (Ronin Publishing, 2004) and *ESP, Hauntings and Poltergeists* (Warner Books, 1986) which was named the 'Sacred Text' on ghosts by *Newsweek*

Loyd Auerbach has been called a 'real-life ghostbuster'.

magazine. Professor Auerbach has also taught parapsychology and related topics for several years in New York and San Francisco and holds an MS in Parapsychology from JFK University (1981), and so he is well qualified to carry out thorough and professional investigations.

What exactly is the Office of Paranormal Investigations and what are its aims and achievements to date?

The Office of Paranormal Investigations (OPI) is dedicated to the scientific investigation and understanding of spontaneous occurrences of psi phenomena.

Founded in 1989 by Loyd Auerbach, MS and Christopher Chacon, OPI was essentially an outgrowth of some of the function of the then-recently defunct Graduate Parapsychology Program of John F. Kennedy University in northern California. At the founding, and since then, OPI as a group has consisted of parapsychological investigators, researchers and other consultants as well as psychic practitioners, who are interested in exploring experiences and situations that people might consider psychic, para-normal, extrasensory, spiritual, or related to these. OPI's primary areas of investigation involve sightings of apparitions (ghosts), unusual happenings in homes or offices or other locations that people have felt are haunted, and poltergeist situations, where there are reported unusual physical effects or movement of objects. In addition, OPI is interested in other forms of psi, such as what has been alternately labelled 'extrasensory perception' and 'extended perception' (including precognition, clairvoyance and telepathy), psychokinesis (mind over matter), psychic healing, reincarnation, near-death experiences, out-of-body experiences, trance channelling and mediumship, and other psychic experiences and practices.

OPI staff investigate the problems reported, first looking for any and all normal explanations before assuming a paranormal one, then they offer recommendations and service with respect to dealing with the phenomena or experiences. While it is effectively impossible to prove the existence of psychic phenomena in these situations given the current state of science and technology, OPI investigators have been successful in assisting people to understand such experiences and, when appropriate, in eliminating the phenomena. OPI does provide a thorough investigation in such cases and an understanding of what is most likely happening, but NO ONE CAN GUARANTEE the removal of such phenomena.

In reality the main contribution OPI makes is in providing educated, credible and ethical help to people who have what they believe are paranormal problems.

Besides investigations into specific phenomena and locations OPI provides consulting services for the media, scientific researchers, business people who wish to consult psychics, attorneys involved in cases with a supernatural element or who may be consulting psychics for jury selection and law enforcement personnel who might be considering calling in a psychic to assist in a difficult case.

How do you reconcile your role as a serious investigator of paranormal phenomena with your professional activities as a psychic entertainer and can you explain what the latter involves?
I first started in magic as a result of a course on magic, 'mentalism and psychic fraud' taught as part of the graduate parapsychology program at John F. Kennedy University when I was a student.

Once in the field of parapsychology I was further encouraged by new colleagues to learn more and get real performing experience and to hone my own expertise in magic and mentalism since this was so often held over the heads of researchers (that they had none).

Through the 1980s and early 1990s, I increased my knowledge of mentalism and psychic entertainment – performing effects in the mind-reading, prediction, and mind over matter vein. It was clear that I got much more out of this form of entertainment than regular magic, and an even better understanding of how people perceive things as paranormal or psychic.

Does your knowledge of cold reading and the allied arts help you to expose fraudulent mediums and identify fake ghost stories?
Knowledge of cold reading frankly does not help with investigations, nor with identifying 'fake' ghost stories. It can certainly help with assessing a purported psychic or medium.

Broader knowledge of the magical arts and mentalism/psychic entertainment absolutely has helped me. But where it's helped is mainly in understanding – how people misperceive, misunderstand and mislabel ordinary (though sometimes rare) events as paranormal ones. In other words, a greater understanding of the psychology of deception and misperception.

In addition, it's also given me an appreciation for there being multiple possible explanations for any reported event – each of which needs to be checked out before coming to a conclusion. There are many ways to saw a lady in half, find a selected card, or even levitate something.

Yes, no question that the knowledge – and more so the performing background – allows me to identify fraud. But as far as detecting fake ghost stories – and here I'm assuming you mean deliberate lying in the telling of a ghost story to me – it's my knowledge of parapsychology that helps the most.

What do you consider has been your most fascinating investigation as far as a haunting or poltergeist activity is concerned and what has it revealed about the nature of the phenomenon?
To me, the most fascinating single investigation was an apparition case

(which is distinguished from a haunting or poltergeist) involving a family all occasionally seeing the former owner of the home they bought. Their son apparently had much more experience, as he reported having daily conversations with the ghost.

The investigation allowed me an opportunity to sit down with a 'ghost' – the boy, only 12, playing translator with the 'ghost' and providing specific details of her life and family (later verified) and then allowing me to interview the 'ghost' about her experience of dying, her experience as a ghost and getting some idea as to why she thought ghosts had clothing on, could be seen at different ages, could or could not move objects, and so on.

That case, and others since then, certainly have convinced me that in some instances people do stick around after death as free-floating consciousness capable of interaction. But more than that, it's clear that we don't alter personality after death – basically ghosts are people, too.

Can you please talk about your investigation of the haunting of the USS Hornet (a haunted WWII era aircraft carrier in Alameda, CA)?

The USS Hornet *is a WWII vintage aircraft carrier with a distinguished history. It was decommissioned in the early 1970s. In 1995, it was brought to a pier at the newly closed Alameda Air Naval Station, where volunteers for a newly formed foundation began repairs and clean-up in order to open it as a museum in 1998. Shortly after the clean-up began, volunteers began seeing apparitions of sailors and officers. Footsteps and voices have been heard when no one else was aboard. Mysterious officers and enlisted men have been sighted (only to have them disappear fairly quickly). Sensations of temperature changes, wind in enclosed spaces and feelings that someone else is present – or touching – have been experienced.*

In 1999, we began our investigations at the request of psychic Stache Margaret Murray, who'd already been working with several of the many witnesses to the phenomena on the Hornet. *With occasional visits over the next few years, we've spoken to dozens of witnesses who have experienced the activity, and have identified more than 25 locations on the ship we might consider 'hot spots', for having multiple reported experiences. I've had my own experiences aboard the* Hornet *as well.*

One of the more unusual facets of the case of the USS Hornet *is that there are several instances of more than one person (in one case, five) having the exact same sighting of a sailor or officer at the same time, and in a few instances the witnesses have seen up to three apparitions at the same time. From descriptions alone, it would appear that there are several dozen apparitions of sailors and officers aboard the ship. It's fairly certain these are the ghosts of people who did NOT die aboard the* Hornet, *as the ship has a low death incidence throughout its working history. Not to mention that workers maintaining the ship when it sat in the shipyards for over 20*

The USS Hornet *is a WWII vintage aircraft carrier.*

years swear it was not haunted at that time (and then proceeded to describe other ships that were haunted in the same shipyard).

We believe, as do most of the on-board witnesses, that these are the spirits of men who did serve aboard the ship, but died in retirement or civilian life after the ship was decommissioned.

The living folks aboard have stated their belief that the ghosts are there to help the ship continue on as a museum, a piece of living history.

We've videotaped interviews with many of the witnesses, and have produced a short documentary, The Haunting of the USS *Hornet,* v.1, *which is still available through my website. We are currently editing all the footage into a more in-depth documentary.*

The museum, the USS Hornet Aircraft Carrier Museum, *is open to the public in Alameda, CA. The ghost stories continue to come in, though our investigations there are infrequent due to a variety of issues.*

Can you tell us something about your work with psychic Annette Martin as far as it relates to ghosts and hauntings?
Annette Martin is an accomplished psychic, with decades of professional experience doing readings for people, as well as working with police in missing persons and homicide cases and participating in research on psychic diagnoses of people's illnesses (with a medical doctor). In addition, she has mediumistic abilities, and I have worked with her in numerous investigations since the early 1990s.

She has demonstrated the ability to communicate with apparitions, and to act as a sort of counsellor to them. In the case of hauntings, she's able to sort out the historical imprint, providing us with information we can verify (not always, as the records are often not complete enough to tell us either way).

Unlike many psychics, she understands the need to eliminate normal explanations first – she even helps with this process. She is more than willing to have her perceptions questioned in order to see if they fit the situation, or are incomplete, or if they might be off somehow.

In one case, apparent poltergeist activity (object movement) was observed only after an apparition had been seen. The family assumed the activity was caused by the apparition. However, based on the family's description of both, and the reactions of the family members to the apparition experience, it seemed something more was happening.

Martin perceived the entity almost immediately, and laughed at his (the apparition's) denial of responsibility for the PK activity. After communicating with the discarnate entity, and discussing it with me, we concluded that the appearance of the apparition (a stranger) to the family was the source of the stress that set off the spontaneous psychokinetic activity.

Martin reported that both she and the entity sensed which of the family members the agent was. The activity was halted by utilizing this information in our discussion with the family, as we would with any poltergeist case. This was followed by communication with the apparition to determine his identity and to 'help him move on' as Martin put it.

The case that best exemplifies Annette Martin's abilities is the Moss Beach Distillery restaurant, south of San Francisco. This is a well-known case with a ghost, commonly called the 'Blue Lady', who has been haunting the place since her death in the early 1930s.

While I've worked with several psychics at the distillery, I've worked there with Martin most frequently, and feel she's made a great connection with the apparition we've come to know as 'Cayte'.

Each time I've visited with Martin with the intention to communicate with Cayte, we've gotten interesting information through Martin, sometimes about the history of the restaurant and town, sometimes about the Blue Lady's life, and often about the ghost's perspective on her decades-long existence in her current state. Some has been verified (where

ESP test: in 1961 twins Terry and Sherry Young, 12, were tested on their ability to 'convey thoughts'. Here, Terry is attempting to communicate the contents of the card she is holding.

we can, the historical information), and other information is similar to what witnesses and other psychic practitioners have described as coming from the ghost.

In addition, Martin's been persuasive with Cayte to get her to co-operate with us. We've been able to use our equipment to detect something whenever Annette is in communication with the Blue Lady.

In February 2005 you launched a new basic Certificate Program in Parapsychological Studies supported by the HCH Institute in Lafayette, CA. Can you describe the contents of the program, the type of students you are hoping to attract and what they will be able to bring to an investigation following their studies?

For those who do want to conduct field investigations after their studies, what they walk away with is a full understanding of how the phenomena of apparitions, hauntings and poltergeists as well as the experiences of people encountering them fit into the broader context of psi phenomena and research. Such things do not exist in a vacuum, and it is unfortunate that the vast majority of ghost-hunters do not comprehend the connection between psi abilities (ESP and PK) and ghosts, hauntings or poltergeists. I've seen some state that psychokinesis does not exist (meaning, among the living) and turn around and describe a situation with moving objects caused by (the mind of) a ghost.

The Certificate Program in Parapsychological Studies is a 60-hour course series providing an overview to the field of parapsychology and the main areas of research and investigation: ESP, PsychoKinesis (Mind Matter Interactions), and Survival of Bodily Death.

Information on the program and course descriptions can be found at www.hypnotherapytraining.com/parapsych.cfm

You are very interested and concerned with media portrayals of the phenomena and the science of parapsychology and have acted as a consultant to various television producers and writers, most notably with shows for the History Channel, A&E and the UK's LivingTV. What is your impression of the media's attitude to the paranormal? They appear to be cynical on principle.

It's not that they're cynical and treat it with disdain, but that so many are ignorant of what the paranormal encompasses, who the real experts are (they so often do not check) and how the phenomena and experiences actually manifest themselves – which is quite different from the general perception that it's weird, scary, and so on, thanks to both religion and fiction (literature, film and television).

The subject is given short shrift for several reasons, some all happening at the same time. Ramp-up time for a series or show may not allow for real research on the part of the writers/producers/production assistants. The budget is generally too low to get the experts involved with more than a phone call – and there's a shortage of experts who know both the subject and television.

While the reality shows can provide some real information, the show itself may often be sensationalistic in order to get at the vast general public that would otherwise only have a passing interest. Fear sells better than education, unfortunately, and most programming is produced for commercial television – meaning the networks who buy the shows are concerned also about sponsors and what sells.

Yes, the networks muck about – mainly in the actual ordering of the show, and their stated expectations. This is hardly limited to shows about the paranormal. It happens in the movie industry all the time (the executives changing the story/plot/characters because of their own expectations of what the public will 'buy').

Often the production people have no real opinion either way as to whether the phenomena are real. Some of the production people are clearly sceptical, but are producing what the networks ask for anyway. The thing to remember is that this is SHOW BUSINESS.

As to whether the media has 'assumed the role once taken by the scientific community', the media has certainly not taken over assessment of psychic phenomena in any sort of way like science has. However, the viewing public seems to accept the often skewed (and sometimes downright wrong) portrayals of the paranormal because the show is labelled as 'reality' or a 'documentary'.

CHAPTER SEVEN

POSSESSED
POSSESSIONS

Before the advent of online auction houses such as eBay, amateur treasure-hunters had to scour out-of-the-way antique shops or sift through cobwebbed attics and basements full of other people's junk in the hope of unearthing a priceless painting or a valuable ornament that the current owner would hopefully part with for a small sum.

But now every bargain-hunter sees themself as an amateur antiques expert and every seller prices their bric-a-brac as if they are family heirlooms.

Some shrewd sellers have even come up with a novel method of getting an edge on their competitors in the potentially lucrative online auctions. They claim that their item, be it a doll, a painting or even a games console, is haunted. Many are clearly trying it on, or have their tongues firmly in their cheeks, but to read some of the descriptions and the earnestness with which the seller states their case one has to wonder.

Are the attics and basements of the US and Europe being emptied of genuine possessed possessions? And if so, does the legal term *caveat emptor* (let the buyer beware) now assume a new meaning?

Arguably the most fascinating and unsettling items on offer are the battered dolls and eerie paintings which must surely give even the most sceptical buyer cause to pause and wonder.

PORTRAIT OF A KILLER?

In 2003 a Florida couple listed a macabre oil painting for sale on eBay entitled 'Stricken Life' which was said to have been the work of a wife-murderer who later committed suicide. It was a portrait of an anguished-looking young man smartly dressed in shirt and tie with blood splatter to one side of the canvas and the spookiest part of the matter, say the owners, is that a second face can be seen in the blood and it's screaming!

On the reverse was attached an equally unsettling self-penned poem:

SCRAPING THE SIDES, RUNNING THEN SLOWING TO A CRAWL – REAJUSTING (sic) THE PACE NUMEROUS TIMES REAPING AND SOWING THIS ROTTEN CROP. TRAFFIC SIGNS LEADING ME TO THE MESSIA (sic) OF RED LIGHTS. STRUCK BY A NOTION TO BURY THE LIVING AND SAVE THE DEAD . . .

Knowing that many would laugh into their laptops at such a loopy story the buyers added a lengthy description, explaining how the painting came to be in their possession and assuring potential bidders that they would provide a complete provenance with the work, 'including signed and NOTORIZED depositions by my wife and I, a local publication's account of the night of the murder-suicide, a copy of the release we had to sign before we could purchase the house, ALL pertinent names and information, as well as anything else we can come up with that pertains to this subject.'

They claim that it was one of the items left behind by the former owner of their new home, which they had purchased at a greatly reduced price because it was rumoured to be haunted. He was the son of a Cuban national who had lived in the house since the mid-1970s. The only other facts that they knew about him, or that they were prepared to divulge online, was that his name was Harold, he had been born in 1949 and he killed his bedridden wife with a shotgun after he had been diagnosed with brain cancer and would not be able to look after her. The sellers take up the story:

'Our initial thought was to get rid of the painting, but our teenage son thought it was "cool". So on the wall it went, along with an interesting story for our friends. Then the strange sounds in the night started. Always in the night, when it was the darkest. My wife and I were in the master bedroom. It was after midnight, and it was our third night in the new house. I had just dozed off when BOOOM!!! the explosive sound of a shotgun blast jerked me awake. SERIOUSLY. My heart about to explode out of my chest, I sat up in bed. My wife still slept. After securing the house, I came back to bed, thinking it was a dream. Several hours later I was awakened again by the most ungodly howling I had ever heard.'

This was their dog. When the husband went to see what was troubling it he found the dog howling at the painting. Disturbed and unable to sleep, he took the painting down and locked it in a closet. Then a couple of nights later his wife woke screaming. She said she had seen a woman in a wheelchair at the end of the bed. But there was no sign of her when the husband finally rubbed the sleep out of his eyes. Then the electrical problems began. Every bulb in a chandelier in their living room burst, the TV would turn itself on and a woman's voice could be heard calling from the master bedroom.

It was then that they decided to list the portrait on eBay, the only picture 'Harold' is thought to have painted. The whereabouts of the painting are not known and the successful bidder's name has never been disclosed, but the former owners should be getting a good night's sleep from now on.

THE HAUNTED PAINTING

Haunted paintings have been the subject of several traditional Victorian ghost stories in which the main protagonist becomes transfixed by a picture which appears to have a life of its own. Whenever the owner returns to admire his purchase he is convinced that the figures have moved. Such stories have become a cliché, so when buyers saw a painting advertised as haunted on online auction house eBay in February 2000, many must have thought it was a joke. But the anonymous owners, a couple from California, had the last laugh when it sold for over a thousand dollars. The question that remains unanswered though, is whether this was a genuine paranormal artefact, or merely a clever sales pitch. The picture depicted two children and, although there was very little remarkable in the subject or the manner in which it was painted, the seller claimed in their sales pitch that it possessed a distinctly singular quality.

'When we received this painting we thought it was really good art. A "picker" had found it abandoned behind an old brewery. At the time we

wondered a little why a seemingly fine painting would be discarded like that (today we don't!)

One morning our 4-year-old daughter claimed that the children in the picture were fighting and coming into the room at night. Now, I don't believe in UFOs or in Elvis being alive, but my husband was alarmed. To my amusement he set up a motion-triggered camera for the night.

After three nights there were pictures. After seeing the boy seemingly exiting the painting under threat we decided that the painting had to go.'

The only clue to the origin of the mysterious picture, which is thought to date from the mid-1960s to the mid-1970s, are the words *The Hands That Resist Him* inscribed in pencil across the back.

The sellers felt it necessary to add a disclaimer, either to indemnify themselves against possible future litigation in the event of supernatural phenomena or perhaps to make it more appealing.

'By bidding on this painting you agree to release the owners of all liability in relation to the sale or any events happening after the sale that might be attributed to this painting. This painting may or may not possess super- natural powers that could impact (on you) or change your life. However, by bidding, you agree to exclusively bid on the value of the artwork with disregard to the last two photos featured in this auction, and hold the owners harmless [sic] in regard to them and their impact, expressed or implied.'

This was sufficient to encourage a flurry of inquiries which seems to have set the sellers on the defensive. Their response was:

'To deter questions in this direction, there are no ghosts in this world, no supernatural powers, this is just a painting and most of these things have an explanation, in this case probably a fluke light effect.

The Hands That Resist Him: *a disquieting title for an unsettling painting.*

'I encourage you to bid on the artwork and consider the last two photographs as pure entertainment and please do not take them into consideration.'

But several potential purchasers reported that the power of the painting extended to their own computers after viewing it online.

'Seven emails reported strange or irregular events taking place when viewing this image,' the seller reported after the sale had closed, 'and I will relay two suggestions made by the senders. First, not to use this image as the background on [your] screen and second, not to display this image around juveniles or children.'

So who paid more than a thousand dollars for an otherwise unremarkable painting? Who else but a shrewd art dealer who knew a good investment when he saw one.

There is a postscript to this story. Following the sale the BBC became interested and managed to track down its artist, Bill Stoneham.

He explained how he came to create such an unsettling picture.

'When I painted The Hands That Resist Him *in 1972 I lived in an old stage-coach station deep in the woods of the Matilija surrounded by 600-year-old oak trees and a stream filled with ancient fossils. I used a family album photo of myself at age five in front of our Chicago, Illinois apartment. The hands are the "other" lives. The glass door, the thin veil between waking and dreaming. The girl-doll is my imagined companion, the ally or guide of Joseph Campbell's* The Hero's Journey. *Some of what I paint resonates in other people, opening their inner door, or basement.'*

GHOST IN A BOTTLE

Without doubt the most unusual spooked item to be listed online has to be the 'ghost in a bottle' auctioned on eBay in December 2004 which a national newspaper claimed had aroused the interest of an agent representing the singer Michael Jackson. Whether Jackson put in the winning bid is not known as the buyer's identity was never revealed.

The bottle was the property of retired mill worker John McMenamin from Spamount, County Tyrone, Northern Ireland, who discovered it cemented into a bricked-up window of his reputedly haunted mill house, but held on to it for twenty-five years before deciding to cash in.

It was described as being at least a hundred years old and was said to contain the imprisoned spirit of a ruthless landlord who had committed suicide after getting a young girl pregnant and then abandoning her to her fate. Angry locals then hounded him to his death. Apparently a local priest had failed to exorcize the ghost from the house, but had managed to force it into the bottle, presumably by promising the disembodied drunkard that stronger spirits awaited him in the bottom of the bottle.

Incredibly, the story caught the imagination of a Northern Irish radio presenter who tracked down and interviewed McMenamin's sister, Marie Maguire, who told the listeners that the bottle contains black dust and is sealed with a page of the Bible. She revealed that when her family moved into the house they knew it was haunted – indeed, that was why the previous occupants had left. Maguire went on to describe childhood experiences, including 'waking up, screaming that somebody was looking at me in bed'. Her brother had reported something coming up the bed 'like a cat's paws'. She concluded by saying that the family wanted the purchaser to treat this 'genuine Irish ghost in a bottle with respect'.

VOODOO DOLLS

There are now so many 'haunted dolls' for sale on eBay that they have their own listings category. Some dealers specialize in these novelties and curiosities which vary from battered, blank-eyed babies that would send any kiddie screaming to its mummy, to sweet old lady dolls designed to serve as surrogate grannies. Some sellers claim that they created their dolls to capture the spirit of a loved one or a friendly ghost which they now offer as house guests for those in need of companionship or protection. But even the cutest come with a warning that they are not to be given to children or people of a nervous and imaginative disposition. The following is typical of those on offer.

'Granny is extremely active and looking for a new home.

My grandmother always collected dolls, and as a child I never knew why I wasn't allowed playing with her "special" dolls, until they were given to me after her passing two years ago.'

According to this seller her dolls become animated after dark, talking and laughing with each other, which the new owners might find unsettling if they are not prepared for it. She claims to have captured the secret life of the dolls on infrared video and EVP recordings (ethereal sounds beyond the range of the human ear). The pride of her collection contains the spirit of a 92-year-old widow named 'Granny' for whom she provides a biography. The old lady was said to be a kindly 'wise woman' who kept a garden to raise vegetables to feed the needy and herbs to cure ailments until she was cruelly murdered by an intruder.

After her death the seller's grandmother and an aunt who was a medium made the doll in the old lady's image right down to the moles on her face and a miniature copy of her wedding ring. Her clothes too were copied from those she had worn on the last day of her life. Revealingly, no mention is made of the method by which the spirit was summoned and bound in the doll's body, but we do get a list of 'Granny's' likes and dislikes and of her nocturnal activities.

'*I hear Granny at night rocking back and forth in her rocking chair, I have found her moved in different positions, sometimes it looks like she is trying to stand, but can't get up by herself. I have seen her as a full-bodied apparition. She looks through my kitchen cabinets, moving dishes around and moving things in one place to another . . . I have heard her humming and whistling, she starts about 1:00am and can go for hours sometimes.*

'*I have found Granny in different rooms from which I put her, and moved from one place to another. Sometimes the look on her face turns from a smile to a frown. I have tried to do EVPs on Granny, but it seems to mess up the tape in the recorder. I don't think she cares too much for modern conveniences. Granny is a LOVING lady, who wants a family to look after. She loves children and animals. She needs a good home, where she can stay and be needed and loved, for the wonderful woman she is.*

'*If you feel a strong connection or bond to Granny then please bid, you could be the one destined to watch over her. Let her help you and watch over you as well. Please Remember: Do not let anyone touch Granny until she is used to you and her new home!*'

The seller shrewdly adds a warning intended for those who might demand their money back if the dolls don't perform on command.

'*My dolls are not "evil". Some have more attitude than others, they have their own unique personality because they were all living, breathing individuals at one time or another.*'

It is evident from the buyers' responses that they entered into the spirit (sic) of the sale and treated the dolls as nothing more than New Age novelties. One buyer wrote of a doll she had bought called Teena:

'It turns out she is quite a little talker . . . she calls us mom and dad. It's really cute . . . We found out there is another spirit in our home that she does not like. She gave us his name and everything. We thought there might have been another one there but we didn't know for sure . . . she's going to help us try to get rid of him . . . and oh, she scares the dog a lot.'

Others wrote to tell of doors which locked by themselves, computer breakdowns, lights switching on and off and fleeting sightings of the spirit leaving its host!

THE DIBBUK BOX

The whole subject of 'haunted' possessions invites a healthy dose of scepticism, but it is worth noting that one item has attracted so much attention that it has become the subject of a website devoted to uncovering its mysterious origins.

In September 2001 it is claimed that among the items included in a house clearance sale in Portland, Oregon was a box containing an evil spirit known in Jewish mythology as a 'Dibbuk'. The former owner was said to be an elderly Jewish immigrant who had been the sole surviving member of her family to be liberated from a Nazi concentration camp in Poland. With no reason or desire to remain in her own country after the war she emigrated to America with her only remaining possessions – a small trunk, a sewing case and the Dibbuk box.

It was her granddaughter who had organized the sale and who related the story of the cabinet to a prospective buyer. She confided that the old lady had kept it locked and out of the reach of curious children. When asked what it contained she would spit three times through her fingers and mumble something about a 'Dibbuk' and 'keselim'; the granddaughter was unfamiliar with both words.

Her dying wish was that the box should be buried with her, but orthodox Jewish tradition forbade that so it was included in the sale.

It was listed as an antique wooden wine cabinet, although one of its subsequent owners has speculated that it was too small to contain wine bottles and glasses would not fit in the rack. However, it may have had a perfectly innocent origin as a liquor cabinet in which could be stored a decanter, shot glasses and tumblers. Or it may have been a container for sacred religious scrolls such as would be needed by a persecuted people who could not worship openly at a synagogue. Inside were two pennies dated 1928 and 1925, two locks of hair bound with string (one fair and one dark), a small statuette engraved with the Hebrew word SHALOM (peace), one dried rosebud, a golden wine cup and a black cast-iron candlestick holder with octopus legs.

The buyer stored it in the basement of his furniture store where he intended to refurbish it as soon as he found some free time. But before he could do so, he became uncomfortable in its presence and decided to sell it on. Apparently, all nine bulbs in the basement had burst and ten fluorescent strip lights, each four feet long, had blown simultaneously. His female assistant had been reduced to a gibbering wreck by 'something' that she had seen and that had locked her in while he had been away. She refused to return to work.

Two weeks later he examined the box more closely prior to working on it and discovered an inscription on the back which he later learned was a Jewish prayer of consecration and protection.

When he presented his mother with the refurbished cabinet as a birthday present she seemed pleased, but within minutes he claims she suffered a stroke which left her partially paralysed. The only means she had of communicating was to write shakily and the message she scrawled was anything but reassuring:

'H-A-T-E-G-I-F-T'.

It was sold this time through eBay to a young man who began to suffer recurring nightmares of being attacked by an old hag. When he gave it to his sister and brother-in-law they returned it complaining of having a strikingly similar dream. The young man in turn sold it to a middle-aged couple who left it on his doorstep soon after without asking for their money back.

Bad luck seemed to plague him from that day on. The lease on his store was terminated without explanation and all the fish in his aquarium died for no apparent reason. While researching the legend of the Dibbuk he fell asleep at his computer and awoke to feel something breathing down his neck. He then watched incredulously as a hulking shadow lurched down the hall.

That did it. The box was back online and bought by a college student in Missouri who was made aware of its unhealthy reputation, but who bought it none the less. Within days he was keeping a journal detailing the uncanny events.

Sunday, 31 August 2003 Over the last week some interesting, though possibly coincidental, items of note have come up. Firstly, I share a house with six other people; we have been taking turns sleeping with the box in each of our rooms.

Two people are now complaining of burning eyes, one is listless and depleted of energy, and another became spontaneously sick. [In retrospect I would say it was allergies.]

A few days after these ongoing annoyances started, the air outside our house was filled with small bugs for several hours (a Friday). [Weird summer stuff?] Last night (Saturday) we discovered that the box, now located in the back corner of the house, had come mostly open, though it had been shut and it seems unlikely that anyone could or would have touched it.

Wednesday, 10 September 2003 *Though it seems impossible to prove that the box is a direct cause of misfortune, we have definitely seen a tidal wave of bad luck. Strange odors now permeate the house, the dumpster out back overflows with trash and decay, one roommate suddenly got bronchitis, and I broke a finger. Several mice have died in the engine of one car, and more electronic devices seem to be dying everyday: Xbox, toaster, t.v., and watches.*

Within months he had re-listed it for sale, adding:

'I don't really want to talk about anything between September and January, so I'll just say that I'm selling the box now for a couple of reasons:

   Around October 6th, I started feeling bad, with trouble sleeping. This problem has persisted through today.

   I live alone now, and as of late I have noticed I have been replacing a lot of burnt-out lightbulbs, and getting many unusual car repairs (transmission fluid was burned out of the reservoir). I've started seeing things, sort of like large vertical dark blurs in my peripheral vision. I smell something like juniper bushes or stingy ammonia in my garage often, and I have no idea what from.

   Most disturbingly, last Tuesday (1-27-2004), my hair began to fall out. Today (Friday) it's about half gone. I'm in my early twenties, and I just got a clean blood test back from the doctor's. Maybe it's stress-related, I don't know.

   Anyhow, for personal reasons I very strongly do not want this box anymore. I hope there's someone on eBay that will take this thing off my *hands. [I would just throw it away in the woods or something, but I know there has been some interest in it in the past.]'*

THE HISTORY OF THE BOX

The previous owner hadn't simply destroyed it either for fear that by doing so he would free the evil within or because he sensed there was something to be gained from passing it on.

In February 2004 the box was acquired for $280 by its present owner, who made great efforts to learn its history. This is what he claims to have discovered:

'The box had been used in séances by the Jewish lady who had emigrated from Poland.

'In November 1938 she and her friends had come to the realization that their harmless parlour game had succeeded in establishing contact with a malevolent entity which desired entry for itself and other evil spirits into our world.

'It would not let the group rest until they had acceded to its demands, so they planned to invoke it one last time and trap it in the box by means of certain spells and incantations.'

The artefacts such as the braids of hair and the pennies were part of the charms that would bind it in the box. But the ritual did not go according to plan and although the entity was eventually subdued it managed to reap destruction on a scale unprecedented until that time. November 10 1938 was the night the Nazis unleashed *Kristallnacht* (the night of broken glass), when their thugs burnt synagogues throughout Germany and smashed the windows of Jewish-owned shops and businesses.

The whole episode has echoes of *Raiders of the Lost Ark* and *The Spear of Destiny* with a touch of H.P. Lovecraft thrown in and it is highly suspicious that the silver-plated wine cup it contains was made by the Leonard Company whose factory was in Oregon, the town in which the Dibbuk box was purchased.

GHOST IN THE MACHINE

The real significance of haunted items is the speed with which such stories are replacing traditional ghost stories and urban legends for a new generation. But who can safely scoff and say that the next time their computer crashes while they are online it isn't because they have inadvertently downloaded a cyber spook? Be very careful the next time you curse your computer – you may be invoking an evil spirit!

We have all damned our computers when they freeze up or crash losing valuable data, but we don't seriously believe that our PCs are possessed. But there are frustrated users who would swear on a stack of Bibles that their hard drive is haunted.

Down south in God's own country, Savanagh, Georgia, the Reverend Jim Peasboro regularly takes to his pulpit to preach against that spawn of Satan, the World Wide Web. He warns of how computers have 'opened yet another door through which Lucifer and his minions can enter and corrupt men's souls'.

Peasboro contends that PCs have enough storage capacity to house evil spirits, and that members of his congregation have come into contact with a 'dark force' when they have used their computers. He tells of how happily-married men have been drawn to pornographic websites and 'forced to witness unspeakable abominations'.

Some might argue that it is not Satan who forces these men to explore their dark side but human nature, and that Satan is merely a convenient excuse for them to absolve themselves of the responsibility for their actions.

But it's not only men apparently who have been tempted off the straight and narrow, from the path of righteousness. According to the minister, even God-fearing Christian women felt compelled to visit online chat rooms which have turned them from housewives into foul-mouthed, fornicating sinners.

The minister tells of how one woman wept as she confessed to a feeling of being 'taken over' when online. In this particular case the crusading preacher took it upon himself to fight the good fight.

He visited the woman's house, where the computer 'talked to and openly mocked' him. It even typed by itself, calling Peasboro a 'weakling' and told him that 'your God is a damn liar'.

Then without being instructed it spewed out pages of doggerel, an experience that most of us will be familiar with. But the minister is adamant this was not a simple malfunction. He claimed to have had an expert in dead languages examine the text. The expert asserted it to be a 'stream of obscenities written in a 2,800-year-old Mesopotamian dialect'!

Reverend Peasboro is also confident that many school shootings like the tragedy at Columbine were perpetrated by computer buffs, having 'no doubt that computer demons exerted an influence on them'.

So what is to be done about this invasion? Is exorcism the only answer? According to the Reverend Peasboro there is a less drastic solution.

'Technicians can replace the hard drive and reinstall the software,' he says with confidence, 'getting rid of the wicked spirit permanently.'

Amen to that.

PHANTOM PHONE CALLS

If it is true that ghosts are merely the discarnate spirits of the living and that they possess the same personality that they had in life, then it is to be expected that the recently deceased would try to communicate with us using the telephone or even email rather than by table-rapping and ectoplasmic manifestations favoured by Victorian spooks.

Julia K's 5-year-old son had shown no interest in the family phone until one day when he stopped playing to answer it. Only it wasn't ringing. At least his mother couldn't hear anything. The child picked up the receiver and entered into a lively conversation, then paused to pass the receiver to his mother who was in the kitchen preparing dinner.

'Who is it?' she asked him, wondering if it could have rung while she was too distracted to hear it.

'Grandmom,' he answered.

'What does she want?'

'She wants to talk to you. She wants to say goodbye.'

His mother took the phone, and anxiously put it to her ear, but she heard nothing. She was relieved and uneasy at the same time. Her mother had died five years earlier and she had never talked about the old lady to her son because she felt he was too young to understand about death. He had not even mentioned her name until that moment.

There was no mistaking the voice on the other end of the line which woke 'Michelle' one Sunday morning. It was her father, who she describes as having a great bear of a voice like the actor James Earl Jones who lent his voice to Darth Vader in the *Star Wars* films. She was recovering from surgery at the time and he began by asking how she was feeling. He also inquired whether she had heard of the death of two people they knew, but she hadn't. At least, not yet. Before he hung up he assured her that life would improve for her and told her that she was not to allow the illness to sap her strength or her spirits. 'When I hung up the phone, it was as if I stepped from another level back into this one,' she later wrote. The call had occurred on 13 September – the second anniversary of his death.

COLD CALLING

The following incident sounds like an urban legend, but Terrie, the young lady who reported it to about.com, insists she experienced this herself while working as a temp for an American telemarketing firm.

Telemarketing calls are commonly made by a computer so the salespeople don't have to dial, but if and when the call is answered they have a scripted sales pitch taped to the desk which they are trained to run through before the caller has a chance to hang up. On this particular occasion an elderly man answered and listened patiently while Terrie went through her prepared speech. When she had finished he asked her how much it was going to cost because he and his wife were on social security and had to be careful what they spent.

But as soon as Terrie started to explain she was interrupted by an old woman who called out 'Hello?' Terrie explained that she was talking to Mr Smith, to which the woman replied, 'Miss, I'm sorry, Mr Smith has been gone for three years now. He passed away.'

Unperturbed, Terrie asked, 'Is there someone else there I could have been talking to?' to which the old lady replied, 'No, honey. I'm here by myself. Can I help you with something?'

Terrie must have looked as white as a sheet when she hung up because the following day her supervisor pulled the call logs and dialled the number in case an intruder had answered the phone. But the old woman assured the supervisor that she was alone in the house and she was well.

In fact, it took some time before she was convinced that the salespeople weren't pulling her leg about the old man.

PHANTOM FORERUNNERS

Not all spooky phone calls come from the spirit world. An American visitor to the about.com website, who gave her name only as Barbara, described a phone conversation that made her wonder if she had received a call from the 'twilight zone'.

She was awoken at 4.20 one morning by a call from her brother. He was ringing at that unnatural hour because he was bursting with good news and wanted her to be the first to know he had just got married. The call lasted about five minutes and was overheard by Barbara's husband, who had also been woken by it. A week or so later Barbara met her brother and his new bride at their mother's house and during the conversation she mentioned the phone call. Her brother looked shocked. He insisted he hadn't called her and then asked her what he was supposed to have said. When she finished both the brother and mother confirmed that those were almost the exact words that had passed between them when he had rung the mother at exactly 4.20am.

Phantom forerunners, which precede the real person on a journey, are a well-documented phenomenon, but phantom forerunner phone calls are a rarity. The following was posted on about.com by a lady wishing to be known only as Cian B.

Cian was driving home from work one Tuesday night with her mother when she casually asked how her father was coping with his Tuesday evening computer course. Cian had talked to him on the phone earlier that day when he had called to say he was having trouble with the second assignment (out of three!) because his computer had malfunctioned. Later that night her father asked her how she knew about his problem and she reminded him they had discussed it on the phone just a few hours earlier. He denied it. She must have been mistaken. What he couldn't understand was how his daughter knew about this before he had left for that evening's class. Even he couldn't have known in advance that he was going to be given three assignments as he had missed the previous week's lesson.

CHAPTER EIGHT

POLTERGEISTS

The word poltergeist derives from the German name for a 'noisy ghost', but there is compelling evidence to suggest that in many cases the 'victims' are unconsciously practising a form of psychokinesis, in which an excess of unchannelled mental energy is discharged into the atmosphere affecting electrical equipment and even moving small objects.

That, of course, leaves a number of incidents for which there can be little doubt that a malevolent entity was responsible for the often violent assaults and other disturbing phenomena.

> *'I think a Person who is thus terrified with the Imagination*
> *of Ghosts and Spectres much more reasonable, than one who*
> *contrary to the Reports of all Historians sacred and profane,*
> *ancient and modern, and to the Traditions of all Nations,*
> *thinks the Appearance of Spirits fabulous and groundless.'*
>
> JOSEPH ADDISON, *The Spectator*, 1711

THE ROSENHEIM CASE

In one of the most remarkable incidents of poltergeist activity on record the disturbances were attributed to an 18-year-old girl whose neurotic disposition is thought to have triggered what amounted to a psychic temper tantrum.

In November 1967 Sigmund Adam, a Munich solicitor, was becoming concerned about a number of electrical faults in his office which were threatening to disrupt his business. He was having to buy new fluorescent strip lights every few days when they should have lasted months and the electric meter had registered inexplicable surges of current which also added to his bill. But the electricians he called in were baffled. During tests their voltmeters registered 3 volts when connected to a 1.5 volt battery, which indicated that there was another source of power leaking into the atmosphere. Such a thing was simply impossible. On Adam's insistence the lighting company installed a generator in case the fault was in the power lines and they advised Adam to use bulbs in place of the strip lights. But the power surges continued and the bulbs blew with monotonous regularity. The generator was replaced, but the problems persisted. Then other phenomena began to occur. The next telephone bill that Adam received listed dozens of calls every day to the speaking clock. None of the staff admitted to making the calls and besides, the speaking clock was being dialled up to six times a minute which was impossible as it took at least 17 seconds to dial the number and be put through. Before Adam could figure that one out, the office was besieged by more 'conventional' poltergeist activity. On several occasions a heavy filing cabinet moved of its own accord and pictures spun on the wall as if turned by unseen hands.

Rumours of the disturbances attracted the attention of the national newspapers and as a result of the publicity Professor Hans Bender of

Munich solicitor Sigmund Adam was concerned at the number of electrical faults in his office.

the Institute of Paranormal Research at Freiburg offered to investigate. Bender soon discovered that the disturbances only occurred when clerk Ann-Marie Schaberl was present. He also learnt that the ceiling lights were seen to swing whenever she walked underneath them. But the most remarkable aspect of the case concerned the calls to the speaking clock. Under questioning, Ann-Marie admitted that she had watched the clock obsessively as she was so bored with the work she had been given. It was Bender's contention that she was unconsciously generating psychokinetic energy to an abnormal degree due to her frustration and, as if to prove his theory, the activity abruptly ceased when she left the office to undergo a series of tests at the institute.

Bender concluded that Ann-Marie's intense, neurotic personality had manifested in certain paranormal phenomena and he wondered if it meant that she might possess other psychic abilities which could be scrutinized under laboratory conditions. In the initial tests she showed no signs of such talents, but after the professor raised the subject of a traumatic illness she had suffered for a whole year her scores increased dramatically.

When she returned to Adam's office the activity resumed, forcing him to dispense with her services. Similar disturbances occurred at her next two jobs with apparently tragic consequences. Ann-Marie was blamed for a colleague's death by the other members of staff, although there was no evidence to support their suspicions, and she was forced to move on. Things deteriorated further when her fiancé broke off their engagement, complaining that every time he took her bowling the electronic scoring system would malfunction. It was only after she met and married another man and settled down to raise a family that the phenomena ceased and Ann-Marie was left in peace.

THE PONTEFRACT POLTERGEIST

'Stones fall on to your kitchen floor, as if they had come through the ceiling. Somebody, or something, starts banging on the wall. Things disappear, and reappear somewhere else. Before long, you realize it can't be an earthquake, or Concorde, or mice. It must be something else – something entirely inexplicable and very frightening indeed.'

GUY LYON PLAYFAIR, *This House Is Haunted*, 1980

A large proportion of poltergeist activity may be attributable to surges of psychokinetic energy and in rare incidents, possibly to the unconscious creation of thought forms, but there are several well-documented cases which appear to offer compelling proof of the presence of malevolent spirits.

Anne-Marie Schaberl – the disturbances only occurred when she was present.

In 1966 the Pritchards of Pontefract, Yorkshire were a typical middle-class British family. Mr Pritchard had a good, steady job which allowed his wife Jean to stay at home to look after their two children, 14-year-old Diane and 5-year-old Philip. But their safe suburban life was soon to be violently disrupted. It began innocuously enough with pools of water on the kitchen floor. What puzzled the Pritchards was the fact that there were no splash marks. But as both the children furiously denied having played a prank there was nothing for them to do but mop up and shrug their shoulders. They weren't aware at the time that the unexplained appearance of water on walls and floors is a characteristic feature of a poltergeist attack. But they were soon to get a crash course on the subject of the paranormal.

When more pools appeared the water board inspectors were called in but they could find no trace of a leak. The following days saw more minor phenomena, but before they could be investigated seriously they ceased and the Pritchards went back to normal. They had two years of normality before the phenomena returned, this time centring on Diane.

Loud reports accompanied the smashing of crockery and other ornaments. So loud were these noises that neighbours would gather outside the house and wonder if the normally placid couple were having an all-out domestic spat. Yorkshire people pride themselves on their down-to-earth, commonsense attitude to whatever unpleasant surprises life throws at them, but even the tightly knit community to which the Pritchards belonged was beginning to talk of poltergeists. The children told their friends that Diane had been dragged out of bed by unseen hands and the parents confided to the neighbours that she had been pinned to the floor on several occasions by falling furniture which took both of them to lift off her.

Curiously, despite the damage it caused, all this activity never actually hurt anyone. Even Diane emerged uninjured from the attacks. Only at the end did the spirit turn nasty, dragging Diane up the stairs in full view of her father, mother and brother who tackled the unseen entity, forcing it to loosen its grip on her throat. But in case anyone thought this was the girl's attempt to get attention she was able to show them a set of angry red fingermarks on her neck. And Diane's mother confirmed her story, adding that she had seen large footprints at the bottom of the stairs that day and that the carpet had been soaking wet.

The poltergeist was evidently not content with being a nuisance. Soon after the attack on Diane it decided to scare the family to death by manifesting in the form of a hooded monk. Mr and Mrs Pritchard described seeing a spectral figure in the night framed in an open doorway and several independent witnesses saw shadowy glimpses of what appeared to be a hooded figure in black elsewhere in the house. On one occasion a neighbour claimed to have felt a distinctive presence behind her and when she turned around found herself confronting a tall hooded monk whose face was hidden by a cowl. An instant later it disappeared. The final sighting occurred one evening when Mr and Mrs Pritchard saw a tall silhouette darken the frosted glass of the dining room door. When they looked inside the room they saw a shadowy shape sink slowly into the floor. It was the last incident in the baffling Pontefract case.

Subsequent research has unearthed the fact that the Pritchard house had been built on the site of a gallows where a Cluniac monk had been hanged for rape during the reign of Henry VIII.

In 1980 the writer Colin Wilson, an expert on the paranormal and an avowed sceptic on the subject of spirits, visited the Pritchard family and interviewed other witnesses including their neighbours.

Their testimonies, together with tape recordings of the violent banging noise and contemporary news reports, finally convinced Wilson that this was a genuine case of poltergeist activity by 'an independent entity'. He later wrote, 'The evidence points clearly in that direction and it would be simple dishonesty not to admit it.'

THE PYROMANIAC POLTERGEIST

'The general character of the phenomena is nearly always the same, and it appears incredible that such coincidental happenings could possibly have taken place in all ages and in all parts of the world, had there not been some genuine manifestations behind these reports.'

H. CARRINGTON, *The Story of the Poltergeist Down the Centuries,* 1953

The standard explanation for all poltergeist activity is that it is caused by displaced energy emitting from an emotionally volatile member of the household, usually an adolescent in the midst of puberty. But this cannot account for the life-threatening disturbances that plagued the Gallo family of Orland Hills, Chicago in the spring and summer of 1988.

It was Dina, one of the couple's two teenage daughters, who first became aware that there might be a phantom firebug in their home when she noticed a shower of sparks from an electrical outlet which quickly set a pair of curtains ablaze. She managed to smother the fire before it could take hold and then she called the fire department, but they failed to find a fault. The only clue Dina could offer was the fact that she had heard a strange popping sound seconds before the sparks appeared. The firemen could do little but sympathize with the family and compliment the girl on her alertness, but they were soon to realize that it had not been a freak accident. Something was seriously wrong in the Gallo residence.

Dina was not present at the second and more serious fire which began in an empty room and which inexplicably extinguished itself before the family could race to the scene, leaving scorched drapes, a blackened carpet and the room full of smoke. The next mysterious blaze began in an unoccupied upstairs room and consumed a desk and yet another set of curtains. This time the fire department were called in and undertook a thorough investigation. But again, they could find no logical explanation for the fire. Furthermore, there was an aspect to the blaze that even they could not explain. Why, they wondered, had several objects near to the source of the flames escaped scorching while the desk had not? By now they were seriously concerned for the welfare of the family, who were becoming increasingly uneasy. In an effort to reassure them and get to the bottom of the mystery the fire department called in electrical engineers to check out the wiring and the outside cables in the belief that there might have been a periodic build-up of current. But nothing unusual could be found. It all seemed in order, except for the fact that even after the power had been cut off and all appliances had been pulled out, several sockets started to emit choking smoke.

It was clear that the entire wiring set-up would have to be ripped out and replaced. It was a costly and disruptive cure, but even this did not solve the problem. Now the new sockets emitted sparks. It was at this point that several members of the investigation team began to talk of seeing a white fog of sulphurous fumes which gave them throbbing headaches. But when they brought in sophisticated equipment to measure the levels of carbon monoxide and other poisonous fumes the meters failed to register gas of any kind.

Then on 7 April the sulphurous cloud appeared again, this time in plain sight of several family members who witnessed a long blue flame shooting out of one outlet and scorch marks appearing around others. The climax of this particular display was the spontaneous incineration of a mattress which was later inspected by experts who estimated that the heat which consumed it must have been in excess of 1,500 degrees Fahrenheit (816 degrees Celsius).

The Gallos were desperate and so too was their insurance company, which had paid out on every claim and now faced the possibility that the next claim might be more than they could afford. Reluctantly they agreed to pay for the demolition of the house and the building of a new home from scratch.

Inevitably the story was picked up by the local media, which repeated rumours that fire investigators had consulted psychics and that they had confirmed that the house had been built on the site of three unknown graves. There was also speculation centring on the Gallo's daughter Dina who, it was said, was always in proximity to the fires, as it was a known fact that most poltergeist activity happened around adolescent girls and abruptly ceased when they grew out of puberty. It is true that in this case the phenomenon did die down after Dina grew out of her teens, but surely even the most emotional teen could not cause the appearance of two-feet-high flames and thick miasmas of sulphurous fog, not to mention intense conflagrations in excess of 1,500 degrees Fahrenheit. Insurance investigators are not renowned for their gullibility or their generosity, so it is safe to assume that they made a thorough study of the phenomenon and concluded that there was a genuine claim to settle.

THE BOY WHO SAW GHOSTS

'Poltergeist phenomena are generally supposed by the sceptical to be the work of artful and mischievous children . . . But in many cases which seem to have been carefully observed and reported the

physical effects are of a nature quite incompatible with child agency.
A child may produce strange noises or throw an occasional stone,
but the movement of heavy furniture, or the flinging of missiles
which enter a room from outside when the child is in the room and
actually under observation cannot be explained in that way.'

HERBERT THURSTON, *Ghosts and Poltergeists*

Most of us enjoy being frightened by tales of hauntings, possessions and poltergeists in the safety of a cinema, or while curled up in an armchair reading novels by authors such as Dean Koontz and Stephen King. But what is it like to experience these horrors for real? If the claims of Connecticut housewife and mother Denice Jones are to be believed any family can be caught up in these living nightmares.

Having survived an unrelenting assault by malevolent and spiteful spirits single-handed for several years, she was determined to set up a non-profit-making support group for families plagued by poltergeists and other terrifying phenomena, L.I.F.E. (Living In Fear Ends), which she says has helped numerous people in a similar situation.

Denice also documented her ordeal in a best-selling book, *The Other Side – The True Story Of The Boy Who Sees Ghosts* (New Horizon Press, 2000), in the hope that it would exorcize the fear and frustration her family had endured.

The Other Side reads like a classic case of poltergeist activity, but it appears that the focus of the phenomenon was not the family home but Denice's son Michael, who was five years old when the problems began.

'There were many incidents before we moved to that house,' she explains. 'My son was always afraid of the dark. But he was young and I assumed it was the normal scared of the dark syndrome.'

It appears that Michael had a troubled birth and it was touch and go whether he would survive. During those crucial first weeks of his life he was declared technically dead on more than one occasion. Denice thinks that he crossed over and returned so many times that when he came back he 'left a door open' to the next world.

FAMILY HISTORY

'Our family was not new to strange experiences. Both my parents have seen the dead in their homes, and my childhood home was haunted. My mother would have premonitions. For instance, one day while my parents were in bed, my mother woke up in a panic and told my dad to get dressed as his mother was coming because his dad had just had a heart attack. My father told her to go to bed as she must be dreaming. So she started yelling at him and during this the knock came at the door and it was my grandmother with the news that his dad had suffered a heart attack.

'My father sees spirits sometimes, but not all the time like Mike, though once he saw a woman's face at the side of his bed. He pinched himself to prove he wasn't dreaming and when he knew he was awake, he asked her not to hurt his family. She then disappeared. Shaken, he went downstairs to check out the house only to see the cabinets and refrigerator doors open and slam shut by themselves.

'Perhaps it's not surprising that I was a fearful child and found it difficult to go to sleep at night for fear that there might be something in the dark. I frequently had the sense of being watched. In some sense I feel now I was being ready as a child for what was to come as an adult with my son. I know that sounds strange. But I do think that. I never knew however how serious it would become for my son and family.

'I also had a few experiences later in life that shook me. One time while driving I "saw" myself hit a deer. I thought I was going crazy. I kept hearing a voice urging me to "turn around" and I had flashes of this deer in my headlight, but I disregarded it as a hallucination brought on by *stress or fatigue. I fought this for two miles. Then suddenly it happened just as I had foreseen it. I hit that deer. It was strange, if I had only listened to myself it would not have happened, but at the time I couldn't accept the possibility that this might be a genuine premonition.*

'Another time while I was washing dishes something came over me and I started screaming at my husband to get Kenny, my oldest son, as he was hurt. Kenny was outside playing at the time and nothing had happened. But just as my husband came back inside to reassure me Kenny let out a terrible scream. He had been throwing a pole around and it had landed on his foot. He was in agony and had to be rushed to hospital. This sort of thing happens very rarely, but when it does it freaks me out.'

EARLY SIGNS

Denice is convinced that her younger son Michael inherited this 'gift' as a direct result of his early brushes with death.

'As soon as Michael was able to talk he would look at things that no one else could see. He'd ask who was upstairs talking when there was no one up there. I would brush them away I guess, hoping it would go away. When I remarried I didn't want to alarm my new husband, Bruce, so whenever Michael woke up screaming in the night I would tell him that Michael was afraid of the dark. It was partly true – he was scared of the dark, but he had good reason to be!

'Bruce had two daughters and when one of them asked if she could move in with us we decided we had to move out of our small apartment and find a four-bedroom family house. We couldn't believe it when we found what seemed to be the perfect place and for half the going rate. We thought we'd won the lottery.

'I didn't have any bad feelings at all. I thought it was nice. The upstairs hall was a bit creepy as it was so long and it felt like it did not stop, but the

house seemed ideal and came just at the right time. The other thing we all noticed was the number of rosaries in the rooms. There seemed to be one in almost every room which was odd. At first I thought it was a nice touch, like a blessing on the house, but later I suspected they might have been put there to protect the previous owners from something or maybe they were left by the previous owners to protect the new owners – us.'

THE OLD MAN

The first indication that Bruce and Denice had that something was seriously wrong in the new house occurred one idyllic autumn afternoon shortly after they had moved in. Denice was working in the garden when she heard a piercing scream. Rushing up to Michael's

Mike went downstairs and saw the cabinets and refrigerator doors open and slam shut by themselves.

room, she saw him cowering in the corner muttering something about an old man who had appeared from nowhere and touched him on the shoulder.

'I didn't think it might be a ghost at that time. It was around 4pm, and ghosts only come out at night, or so I thought. Now I know they come at all hours. All I could think was who else might be in the house. I grabbed my son's metal toy truck and ran around the upstairs, my heart pumping, thinking I am going to have to beat someone with a metal truck! When I failed to find anyone in the house and seeing how scared my son still was, I held him and we talked about the man as calmly as we could under the circumstances. Michael said he was crayon-coloured white. And he said that the man had tried to touch his shoulder. Of course, there was no man in the house. I didn't know what to do. I was Catholic and my boys went to catechism. I believed in the other side, growing up in a haunted home and having parents who were different, but just because you believe in such things it doesn't mean you automatically attribute such incidents to apparitions. Who would want to believe that they're sharing their home with the spirits of dead people?

'That night I took my kids to my parents' home because I wanted to talk to my mom. While we were talking we heard a cry from the other room. Michael had seen a sculpture my father had made of his father and Michael had recognized the face as being that of the man who had appeared in his room.

'My father assured Mike that his great grandfather would never hurt him and that he was not to be afraid of him. Great grandfather was an angel who would look after him. This made Michael feel a bit better, but I was very uneasy with the whole idea. Mike was seeing my dead grandfather. I did pray to my grandfather when Michael was born to look over him as I was close to my grandpa. And I gave Michael my *grandfather's middle name so maybe Grandpa was watching. But now maybe he was watching over Mike because he needed protection.'*

TALKING TO THE ANGELS

'It was nice that Mike was okay with this, except a few days later I heard Mike upstairs talking so I went upstairs and he was on his knees on the floor, looking up and chatting away. When I asked him who he was talking to he said they were his guardian angels. After that I took Mike to every doctor I could find from psychiatrists to neurologists, even eye doctors and so on. But none of them could find anything physically wrong so they suggested I consult a psychic.

'He was being hit, scratched and choked in front of us, but by what or whom we couldn't tell. I didn't know what to do. But I knew it was important to record everything. I just wanted answers and I was desperate for help.

'Sometimes Michael would lapse into a comatose-like state and had to be taken to hospital. He would appear to be asleep, but afterwards he could recall what we had been saying while we were watching him. The hospital called in the priest one time when they couldn't wake him. The priest prayed over Mike and he woke up. I was sure it was a spiritual condition, but you just never know as a parent and I was not sure what I wanted. Sometimes I would think a pill could cure him as if it was an illness. But no pill would or could cure Mike.

'The whole experience alarmed me – Mike screaming every night because there was a woman in his room, or a man; someone on the stairs, a little boy running around, a man with a bandana standing in his doorway, his bed jumping up and down, him being scratched and blood coming from it as I sat next to him. He choked every time I put holy water or a cross on him while in those paralyzed states. But it wasn't just Mike who was the target of the phenomena. Our hair was being pulled by unseen entities, something would tug at our feet, objects were moving

on their own in the house, things were disappearing never to be found, electrical outlets blew up when Mike walked past them and a black smoke or fog would hang over them.

'What made my sceptical husband a true believer was when he and I were on the couch downstairs in the living room watching TV and we heard a banging on the ceiling and the kids screaming upstairs. We raced up to see Bruce's daughter and Mike's older brother Kenny standing in the doorway of Mike's room in a state of real fear watching Mike's bunk bed banging up and down on its own while Mike was hanging on to it for dear life. Bruce grabbed Mike and we all ran downstairs. We all slept together that night and we could hear things being smashed in Mike's room. When we got up Bruce opened Mike's door and all his toys were on the floor, many of them smashed to pieces. At that moment I knew we couldn't run. We had to fight. We all felt so alone and in our own little world. But that is what finally convinced my husband that we were dealing with something supernatural.'

UNSEEN ATTACKERS

Denice says that the hardest part was not knowing what they were dealing with as they couldn't see who was hurting Michael. Their only defence at the time was to pray for him.

'It was pretty scary when he was being choked as he would gasp for air and you could see his throat go in. I actually recorded this on tape because I knew people would find it hard to believe otherwise. And there was the time my mother was dragged out of bed by her feet by an unseen entity while trying to protect my son who was staying with her at the time. The ghost had followed him to her home miles away. It was then that I realized that it wasn't our house that was haunted, but rather that Michael was the focus of some malevolent beings.

'Another time, Michael was staying with my parents when something

attacked him and my father stepped in and called on it to attack him instead. He regretted that. The next moment it leapt on him and pinned him to the floor. My dad had the impression it was a big beast like a lion. He was paralysed by the energy emanating out of this thing for a few minutes until it let him go. He was badly shaken and told me that he didn't know how Michael was able to survive such terrifying experiences.'

The Jones family were evidently not the only people to be taunted by the entities in their home. On an occasion when Denice's sister and her children came to stay with them, Denice's young niece ran screaming from the bathroom. Something had turned the water full on in the hand basin and was laughing at her. The children and their mother refused to stay in the house a moment longer.

Then the growling began. It was an ominous, threatening sound which couldn't be traced to any specific spot. That's what made it so unnerving.

As the attacks on Michael intensified, leaving him in a paralysed state for anything between two and six hours, Denice was forced to take him out of school and educate him at home. Life for the whole family was becoming intolerable. The other children wouldn't go to the bathroom alone or take a shower without a parent being present. Whenever they wanted to fetch a drink or snack they would go in pairs. Even Denice was afraid to stay in the house alone when the children were at school and Bruce was at work.

She would sit in her car in the parking lot until it was time to collect the kids, or she would busy herself with chores around town.

INVITING THE INVESTIGATORS

Eventually they turned to a team of paranormal investigators for help. The investigators captured EVP (electronic voice phenomena) and what Denice refers to as 'abnormalities' in several photographs that they took, but she felt they were more interested in using her story to promote themselves and notes wryly that they got themselves a speeding ticket on the way to a TV station. Eventually their relationship degenerated to the point where the Joneses brought in their lawyers to argue their claim over the rights to the material that had been collected and the potentially lucrative story which the investigators wanted to see in print. But Denice was grateful to them for bringing in the local Catholic bishop, who performed the first of several exorcisms which appeared to have reduced the severity of the attacks that Michael was suffering from at the time.

'Watching my son being hit, scratched and choked by unseen entities was as painful as watching a human hurting him, but with the added trauma of not knowing what it was or being able to pull them off. I had to fight back and the only way I knew how was through my faith.'

THE EXORCIST

'Initially I went to my church for help as I had put my kids through catechism there, but they refused to listen to me. I begged them to bless my home, but they told me they do not do that anymore. I felt like I had been slapped in the face. I was angry and upset. So, I wrote to the archdiocese, but received no answer. Then I called them and they told me it would be months before I heard from someone. I begged them to help. I told them it was urgent, that my son was being hurt and we cannot wait any longer. I told them I had medical reports and video evidence, but they were totally unsympathetic and I never heard from them again. Then I was told about a bishop in Monroe. He asked for all the evidence we had and said he would help my son. But I would have to wait another three days after he had studied all the papers and video as

he said Michael would need the exorcism in Latin and he would need to fast for three days to be in a state of grace for that to be effective. When we met I felt so sorry for him. The poor man was thin enough and looked like he could do with a decent meal.

'*He conducted the exorcism in an empty church. Michael sat at the front and was very quiet. He complained of feeling sick and the bishop gave him holy water to drink. He kept looking off to one side as if he could see something there. Later he told me that he had seen a shadowy figure laughing at him. I was very emotional during the ceremony although I didn't understand what was being said. It was all in Latin. There were no histrionics. No demonic voices or special effects like in the movies. It was very dignified and moving. I felt a great sense of love wash over me, but at one point I felt a cold breeze in my face and I caught the smell of roses. Afterwards Michael told me that he had felt the same chill and had also smelt the flowers and that he now felt that everything looked brighter than it had before.*

'*When it was over the bishop said it may take more than one session and that I could call him at any time. He refused to take any money – even a donation. This sense of relief and of a weight being lifted from us only lasted a short time, then it all just went crazy again. Sensitive souls attract spirits and you can't pick and choose what comes in. Mike's psychic gifts made him a torch in the darkness.*'

EVERY HOME HAS ITS SPIRITS

Eventually the family were forced out of the house by the relentless poltergeist activity, but that didn't solve the matter.

'*Every home has its own spirits. Luckily those in the next house were not as mean as those in the first place, but nevertheless it was hard. We moved many times to flee the memories of what had occurred in those houses. But it wasn't until Mike was 16 that he came to the realization that he needed to live with them and even learn from them.*

'By this time we understood that it was Michael's sensitivity and abilities that attracted things to him, or awakened what was already there. A few weeks after we moved into our present home, Mike told me that there was an old lady with long gray hair bending over the counter by the microwave. He described the mother-in-law of the previous owner who I had seen in a photograph they'd left behind. This time Mike was not afraid. The spirits do not scare him anymore and because he has lost a lot of his fear, the negative entities have not been attracted to him and the number of worrying incidents has been dramatically reduced.'

GOING PUBLIC

I concluded my interview with Denice by asking what prompted her to write the book and whether she regretted making her experiences public.

'I had a lot of publicity before the book was published as the result of the investigators who wanted to make themselves famous from our story. I was on national TV shows such as Primetime Live, Unsolved Mysteries *and so on. The next day I opened my door to see news cameras parked in my front yard so I slammed the door and within minutes the investigators were at my house asking why I wasn't co-operating.*

'They told me that the press was saying my son's exorcism was not sanctioned by the Roman Catholic Church. I had the bishop do it because I wouldn't wait for months as the Church wanted me to. They urged me to defend the bishop which I did. I refused to let anyone say what the bishop did was wrong. He helped my son when the Church refused to do so. And this is why I went to the media. But once the story was out, it was relentless. The intrusion into our lives just wouldn't stop.

'The movie The Sixth Sense *came out many months after I did the* *TV shows and newspaper interviews and I was told on many occasions* *by the journalists that they thought the film had been based on my son's* *experiences. It was such a similar story. When Michael saw that film he* *couldn't sit through it to the end though. It was too close to what he had* *been through. It was suggested that I do something about it through my* *attorneys, but I didn't publicize our story to make money. I did it to make* *people aware that they are not alone in this. Other families have shared* *our experiences and suffered as we have done simply because they have a* *son or daughter who is sensitive to the other side.*

'*I did not enjoy the media attention. Some were nice, but others were* *aggressive, intrusive, cynical and mean. I received a lot of support from* *families of different faiths and I still receive letters of support in the mail* *from people. I try to answer all of them personally.*

'*I don't mind sceptics at all. It is hard for anyone who has not been* *through a haunting to believe in such things and to fully understand what* *it is like.*

'*There are many people who wish to see ghosts and experience all sorts* *of paranormal and psychic phenomena. What I'd say to them is, 'be careful* *what you wish for'. As far as the sceptics are concerned, if they went* *through a quarter of what we had experienced they would no longer be* *sceptics and I wouldn't wish that on anyone. So if they are still sceptical* *after reading our story, it only means they had not experienced the power* *of the paranormal. Isn't that a wonderful life? I wish I could say the same!'*

The Phantom Painter

Not all cases of possession are unpleasant or distressing.

In 1905 Frederick Thompson, an undistinguished amateur

English artist, began to paint remarkable pictures in the style of the celebrated Robert Swain Gifford, who had recently died. The two artists had met briefly, but Thompson was not familiar with Gifford's work [see 'Trees and Meadow', below]. It was only when he visited an exhibition of Gifford's work that he saw the similarity between his new creations and that of the dead artist.

While studying one of Gifford's pictures Thompson heard a voice in his head urging him to continue his work. 'You see what I have done. Can you not take up and finish my work?' It was the same voice Thompson had been hearing for the past 18 months which had suggested the subjects he was to paint. Thompson feared he was going out of his mind, but the paintings were far more accomplished than he had previously been able to create and he was even able to sell some of them. In time these came to the attention of an art critic who remarked on the fact that several of Thompson's works were uncannily similar to sketches Gifford had left unfinished at the time of his death. In time Gifford's influence waned, but Thompson retained his new-found skills and gradually gained the respect of the art world.

CHAPTER NINE

EXORCISTS

If ghosts are either residual personal energy echoing in the ether or discarnate earthbound spirits and poltergeist phenomena can be attributable mainly to involuntary bursts of telekinetic energy, is there any compelling evidence for belief in the existence of evil spirits? Or are the cases of demonic possession a symptom of ingrained superstition and the misdiagnosis of serious personality disorders?

DEMONS AND DEVILS

December 11 1937 was a date as infamous as any in the history of warfare for it was the date of the atrocious massacre at Nanking. Hundreds of thousands of innocent Chinese civilians were butchered by invading Japanese troops who were running amok in the wake of the bombing that had razed the sprawling city of wooden buildings to the ground. It was a scene of hell on earth, but in the midst of the carnage and chaos the gates of the underworld were gaping wide for a real demon, a cannibalistic serial killer who had been tracked down to his hideout in a disused grain store. The police had surrounded the building and were determined to see justice done even though his murders seemed almost inconsequential compared to the mass slaughter taking place on the other side of the city.

But this was no ordinary criminal case. The police had been summoned to the scene by Father Michael Strong, the local parish priest who had sent word for them to delay the arrest while he conducted an exorcism. It was Father Michael's unshakable belief that the fugitive, Thomas Wu, had murdered and eaten his victims while possessed by a demon and he was going to drive it out if the authorities and the Japanese bombardment would give him just ten minutes to confront the real perpetrator of those atrocious crimes face to face.

When the police captain arrived on the scene he found Father Michael standing over the cowering naked figure of Thomas Wu, who brandished a knife in one hand. He was in a severely agitated state and looked like a cornered animal who might spring out of his lair at any moment. As the captain's eyes adjusted to the lamp light he caught a glimpse of a sight that must have haunted him to his dying day. Arranged around the walls on wide wooden shelves were the decaying corpses of dozens of Wu's victims. What kind of man could have perpetrated these atrocities? But it was not a man. It was a demon and he was about to reveal his true face, or faces, for the astonished onlookers.

'YOU!' screamed Wu in a voice both the captain and the priest did not recognize even though they had known him since he had been a boy. 'YOU want to know MY name!' At this outburst Father Michael staggered backwards as if the force of the words had dealt him a body blow. Father Michael's exhortations in the name of Jesus had no effect on the grinning, slavering man who seemed to summon up inhuman reserves of strength to draw himself up to his full height and bellow like some wounded beast. 'Get out of here. Get the hell out of here, you filthy old eunuch!'

It took all of Father Michael's faith to remain upright and, his voice shaking with emotion, continue to demand that the unclean spirit depart.

Wu roared a string of expletives at the beleaguered priest which were suddenly cut short when the roof timbers caught alight. It must have been a stray incendiary, or perhaps it was the devil's way of robbing the priest of his prey. The next instant the police captain had grabbed Father Michael and was pulling him from the burning building.

From just a few feet away they watched the flames consume the wooden grain store together with their quarry and the mutilated bodies of his victims. But Thomas Wu did not go quietly and neither did the spirit which possessed him. A face appeared at the window, a hideous, contorted face which Father Michael later described as having 'the thumbprint of Cain' upon it. From within they heard a hideous mocking laugh and then they witnessed a shocking sight. Wu's features dissolved and in their place a succession of faces appeared as if the demon's former hosts were being released in Wu's death agony. They were the half-remembered faces of Father Michael's nightmares. Others he thought he had seen in old churches. Some were male, some female. They were of every race and nationality, but they shared one characteristic. They were all evil. Then the window went black and the wooden structure collapsed in a sheet of flame and smoke. It was too much for the ageing priest. He clutched at his chest in agony and collapsed. But he lived to tell the tale.

Such a scene might sound like a script from a horror movie, but this event is said to be as true as the massacre of Nanking and not untypical of the confrontations experienced by real exorcists who claim to be fighting the good fight to this day.

(Source: *The Diaries of Father Strong* as reproduced in *Hostage to the Devil* by Father Malachi Martin)

THE EXORCIST

Author Peter Blatty based his best-selling novel *The Exorcist* (which became the basis for the controversial film of the same name) on a real case of alleged demonic possession which had occurred in a suburb of Washington DC in the first four months of 1949. According to a report in the *Washington Post* that year, a 14-year-old boy by the name of Robbie Mannheim had exhibited classic symptoms of possession, specifically spontaneous body wounds, involuntary bouts of abusive language and a distinct change of personality after trying to communicate with the spirit world using a Ouija board. Doctors who examined Robbie could find no medical reason for his behaviour, nor for the physical cuts. The best explanation they could offer was that he was suffering some form of mental breakdown because he could not accept the recent death of a favourite aunt. According to their theories his persistent denial might have produced a number of psychological disorders ranging from automatism (involuntary physical actions), obsessive-compulsive disorder (irrational fears or paranoia and possession) and even Gilles de la Tourette's syndrome (which produces physical and verbal tics, along with foul language). But such rational explanations did not satisfy the family, who brought in a Catholic priest in the belief that their son was possessed by a demon. How else could they explain the scratches on his chest which spelt out the words HELL and SPITE, or the fact that he taunted them in Latin – a language he had never studied?

While the boy writhed in his hospital bed the priest began the Roman ritual of exorcism, but the struggle was cut short when the boy lashed out with a loosened bed spring, causing a deep gash down the priest's right arm that required more than a hundred stitches. Undaunted, another priest took his place and for twenty-four successive nights the two priests – Father Walter Halloran and Father William Bowdern – prayed at the boy's bedside. On the final night, Robbie opened his eyes and said calmly, 'He's gone.'

The Catholic Church has distanced itself in recent years from the practice of exorcism and no longer endorses it, while a 1972 Church of England report condemned the practice as 'extremely dubious'. In a notorious British murder case in 1974 in which a mentally unstable individual, Michael Taylor, killed his wife after being subjected to an all-night exorcism his lawyer criticized the group who had agreed to exorcize him by saying that they had fed 'neuroses to a neurotic'.

But despite such criticisms there are those who still believe that good and evil are constantly at war for the possession of our souls. Father Halloran, who took part in the Robbie Mannheim case, recalled a conversation he had with Father Bowdern at the time in which the latter observed, 'They will never say whether it was, or it wasn't [a genuine case], but you and I know it. We were there.'

THE REAL EXORCIST

'I do not fear Satan half so much as I fear those who fear him.'
St Teresa of Avila

During his sixteen years on the front line fighting crime in the South Bronx, New York City cop Ralph Sarchie has seen the darkest side of human nature, but he claims that tackling murderers, drug addicts and armed robbers is easy compared to the fiends he faces off duty. When Sergeant Sarchie hangs up his gun at the end of his shift he arms himself with what he believes to be the only effective defence against the forces of evil – a vial of holy water and a crucifix, for Sarchie is a real-life exorcist – and the devil had better watch his step when this guy is on his tail. 'As devout Catholics we take Jesus' biblical injunction to "cast out demons in my name" literally,' he says with obvious pride.

EXORCISTS AT WORK

Sarchie's colleagues at the 46th Precinct used to tease him unmercifully, but this latter day 'night stalker' has had the last laugh. His most dramatic 'cases' are now the basis of a best-seller, *Beware of the Night*, which reads like a hardboiled crime novel, but with demons cast in the role of the bad guys. The book has earned him a reputation as a courageous latter-day crusader among America's Christian right who believe the Devil is behind every evil act on earth, but it has brought condemnation from those who fear that in blaming society's ills on a mythical villain we are absolving ourselves of the responsibility for our own actions and risk being dragged back to the Dark Ages.

Sarchie's critics point out that while there is compelling anecdotal and photographic evidence for the existence of ghosts, no one outside a lunatic asylum has claimed to have seen the Devil since the Middle Ages. They cite the fact that publication of the book also contradicts Sarchie's own edict prohibiting anyone from discussing such experiences because to acknowledge the existence of a demon is to empower it, to which he replies that the public needs to be warned about the growing threat from the Devil and his disciples. He quotes Father James LeBar, one of four exorcists currently serving the Archdiocese of New York, who has stated that exorcisms increased from none in 1990 to 'over 300 hundred' by the turn of the millennium. Each year there are said to be between 800 and 1,300 authorized exorcisms around the world.

In an interview for the Christian network Enigma Radio in October 2005 he offered his theory as to why demonic possessions are on the increase. He believes that more people are 'dabbling in the occult' than ever before, which makes them a target for roaming malevolent entities. The only defence, he says, is a strong religious faith and a diet of daily prayer. According to Sarchie, who describes himself as a devoutly religious man, the battle lines were drawn after the

Are too many people dabbling in the occult?

September 11 attacks and we are now entering the so-called 'end time' prophesied in the Bible when it will not be enough to sit on the fence and watch the apocalyptic struggle from the sidelines.

POLICEMEN OF THE SPIRITUAL WORLD

Sarchie claims to have assisted at more than twenty exorcisms where he acted as 'the muscle', restraining the possessed person while a Catholic priest performed the rite. But with his mentor Father Martin recently deceased, he is finding it increasingly difficult to persuade a member of the clergy to agree to perform an exorcism, a situation he sees as symptomatic of Satan's influence in the priesthood! Priests, he reasons, are the 'policemen of the spiritual world' and he points out that even Jesus performed exorcisms. He argues that Satan has got his hand in everything 'from politics to religion' and yet 'many priests and even bishops of the Catholic Church don't believe in the Devil'. Protestant clergy are no help either, he says, as they only offer what they call 'a deliverance' which involves praying to God to intervene in cases of poltergeist infestation or possession. Only Catholic priests are authorized to confront evil in person, so to speak, so Sarchie now offers to take on the heavies himself.

He denies the accusation that he is a self-righteous 'religious fanatic' and admits he is 'anything but holy', but he is deadly serious about his one-man mission which he refers to as 'the Work', to distinguish his calling from his career.

And he sincerely believes that his experience in interrogating killers and rapists has prepared him for the 'real struggle' with an adversary who is more sly and seductive than any conman he has ever confronted.

STAGES OF POSSESSION

It is Sarchie's understanding that the aim of the demonic is to create 'self-doubt and emotional turmoil which eats away at their prey's willpower paving the way for possession'. The first stage of possession, he says, is obsession, which involves the individual brooding on irrational fears, indulging in aberrant behaviour, indulging in a morbid preoccupation with violent crime, or dabbling in the occult such as experimenting with Ouija boards.

'There ought to be a law against these evil, occult toys. I can hear some of you out there saying, "Hey, I used a Ouija board and nothing happened." Consider yourself lucky, then. It's like playing Russian roulette. When you put the gun to your head, if you don't hear a loud noise, you made it. Same thing with the board: The more times you pull the trigger, the more likely that on the next shot your entire world will go black.'

Such obsessions, he says, aim to destroy a person's spirituality from the inside.

In Sarchie's supernatural scheme of things the second stage, 'oppression', will see the entity assault the senses with hideous animal shrieks, loud noises and other inexplicable phenomena, all of which are intended to unnerve them and break down their resistance like a city under siege. These attacks tend to occur around 3 am when their victims are at their lowest ebb, the same time that most suicides take place.

'Not only do satanic powers often do things in threes, to show contempt for the Holy Trinity, but their terrorist strikes frequently occur at 3am. This is another insult to God, whose Son Jesus Christ died on the cross at 3pm. The demonic will do the opposite of anything holy, so they like to

attack at exactly the opposite hour – with supernatural phenomena you might call miracles in reverse.'

The third and final stage is full physical possession when the victim becomes subject to the greater will of the demon. The victim will appear normal until the entity is challenged to reveal its true nature during the exorcism, and then Sarchie says he can see 'it', meaning evil, in their eyes.

PURIFICATION THROUGH FASTING

In preparation for the rite an exorcist must fast for three days to purify himself, which means that he will not be in the best condition for what is often a long and exhausting struggle. Aside from the mental and emotional strain, he invariably has to subdue the possessed person who may have acquired exceptional physical strength, which also happens to be a phenomenon in cases of certain mental disorders.

One rite took two gruelling hours to cast out the 'unclean spirit' and left the muscular cop shaking and exhausted as if he'd been 'working out in the gym'. Such experiences do not appear to have dampened Sarchie's enthusiasm for the work or to have dented his conviction that 'God doesn't let people take on more than they can handle', which he offers as the only explanation for the fact that in a previous attack it had taken five people to hold the victim down, but miraculously he was able to do it alone on this occasion.

According to Sarchie, demonic entities 'can level a house in a second. The amount of power even the lowest demon has is stunning', but they are subject to the limitations imposed on them by God who 'uses them to test us'.

So how do we combat this unseen threat?

'Direct confrontation is the only way. Otherwise it's just human Will against the demonic and we know where that can lead . . . I try to take myself out, so I say, "You are commanded in the name of Jesus Christ" and not "I command you". We don't have the power over the demonic. It's all in God. We're being attacked all the time, but spiritually aware people know who is attacking them and are able to defend themselves despite their fear.'

This self-appointed saviour clearly considers himself one of the 'spiritually aware' and believes he is able to distinguish between a ghost and one of Satan's soldiers.

Ghosts, he says, are the spirits of the deceased while demons were once angelic beings who have lost their supernatural graces, but not their powers. They range from violent brutes which grunt and growl like the beasts of the earth to those which attack using their intellect. It is Sarchie's assertion that a demon can't masquerade as a friendly spirit for long and must eventually reveal its true nature. At this point the victim will be too weak to help themselves so only an exorcist can compel the entity to depart. Sarchie's strategy is to bind it, meaning that he commands it not to interfere in a manner which sounds suspiciously like that practised by medieval magicians. Evidently the line between magic and religious ritual is a very fine one indeed.

'I don't want to see manifestations or phenomena,' he says. 'I don't want to smell things that will make me vomit and see things thrown around. Once I got a whiff as I was tying them down and vomited. I had fasted for three days before so I was dry heaving. Very unpleasant.'

He then breaks contact with the subject of the cleansing so as not to be drawn into a dialogue. From this point on he assumes that anything issuing from the mouth of the victim comes from the demon and so ignores any 'pitiful pleas for help'.

He also refuses to look into the eyes of the host for fear of being distracted from his task, claiming that the demon will interpret his gaze as a challenge. This may be a good tactic if the attack is genuine, but if the victim is suffering from any form of psychological disorder, ignoring their distress and avoiding eye contact while berating them for being possessed by an unclean spirit might be counterproductive to say the least.

DEMONS AND STOCKHOLM SYNDROME

Often the host will see the exorcist as a threat rather than as a rescuer – someone who is intending to cause them psychological and physical pain – and will vigorously resist all efforts to drive the demon from their body. It is Sarchie's belief that the parasitic nature of the entity can even create a psychological state similar to Stockholm Syndrome in which kidnap victims identify with their abductors, meaning that the victim may resent his interference. Of course, if the individual was suffering a psychological rather than a psychic disorder then their resentment and resistance will be more than justified.

A typical case will begin with a frantic phone call from a desperate spouse or family member claiming that their beloved husband, wife or child has undergone a drastic personality change. But Sarchie says he can only intervene when invited to do so by the person suffering from the alleged possession and obviously no demon worth the name is going to allow their host to do that, unless they're spoiling for a fight. However, permission isn't required if their home is the scene of what he calls an 'infestation', meaning that the possessed person has become the focus of demonic (i.e., poltergeist) activity and is likely to cause harm to himself or to other members of the family.

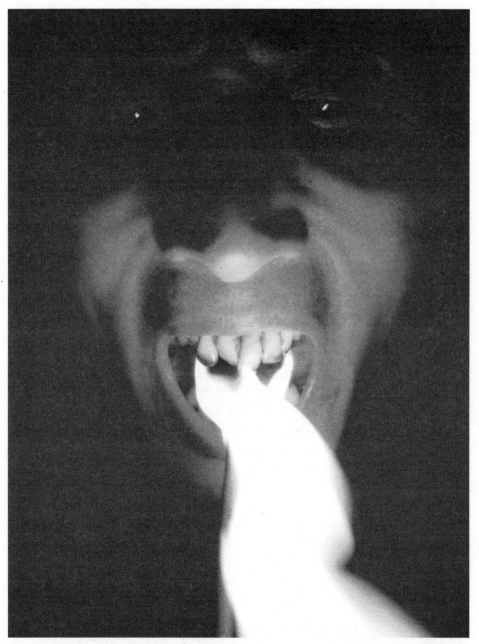

'Demons range from violent brutes which grunt and growl like the beasts of the earth to those which attack using intellect'.

THE HALLOWEEN EXORCISM

Of the 20 cases of alleged demonic possession that Sarchie has had to deal with he considers the most harrowing to be the one he faced on Halloween night in 1991. It began when his late partner, Joe Forrester, a polygraph examiner in the legal aid department, received a phone call from a Catholic priest in wealthy Westchester County, north of New York City. Joe, whose balding head framed with brown hair led to him being mistaken for a Benedictine monk, was no soft touch when it came to the supernatural. A former Vietnam veteran, he boasted what Sarchie called a 'built-in bullshit meter', meaning that he knew when he was being conned.

But Sarchie claims that this incident had all the hallmarks of a genuine case of demonic possession. A young suburban housewife and mother, Gabby Villanova, had been pestered by a sorrowful-sounding spirit by the name of Virginia who claimed to have been murdered on her wedding night and was seeking to be reunited with her family. Her fiancé had been falsely accused of the murder and had taken his own life while awaiting trial. When pressed by Gabby to name the guilty party the grieving spirit is said to have wailed, 'Must not say!' Evidently its strategy was to draw its intended victim in by spinning a tale of unrequited love as histrionic as a Victorian melodrama in the hope of eliciting sympathy.

Having ensured Gabby's attention, 'Virginia' then manifested in broad daylight while Gabby was alone in the basement. This is what she told her rescuer after the 'spirit' had been exorcized and she had recovered her composure:

'My attention was drawn to a large mirror we have hanging there. And in it I saw Virginia. Again she said, "Parents, help." Then she told me she had been in a finishing school abroad and had followed her parents here. In

quaint old-fashioned speech she said, "What manner of place is this?" On looking around the room and at me she asked, "What manner of dress is this?" I answered, "This is how we dress in the 1990s," but she insisted that the year was 1901. I felt no fear of her, and we had a lengthy conversation.'

The next time it literally took possession of Gabby against her will.

'I felt her presence and said, "If you wish to speak do not enter me. I will relate whatever you say." She paid no attention and immediately entered me. When she came into me her voice was stuttery and she kept saying, "Parents, help."'

Sarchie notes that 'a demon has no respect for human pleas, requests or even orders for it to depart unless the command is made in the name of Jesus Christ.'

At the time Gabby was sharing her home with a middle-aged woman by the name of Ruth and Ruth's 25-year-old son Carl, who had become engaged to Gabby's daughter. Ruth was said to have 'witnessed' telepathic conversations between Gabby and 'Virginia', whose emotional outbursts were becoming more hysterical. Ruth, of course, only heard Gabby's side of the conversation. Nevertheless she too was allegedly taken in by the heartbreaking story and wept at the sad and sorry tale.

In this particular case Sarchie considered the entity to be far more persuasive and subtle than any professional con artist that he had encountered in his career with the NYPD.

Sarchie says that Gabby's suspicions should have been aroused by the numerous coincidences between her own life and strikingly similar episodes in the spirit's life story. But she allowed her maternal instincts to be exploited.

POSSESSION OR SCHIZOPHRENIA?

Sarchie's staunch Catholicism has clearly coloured his perception of definitions of good and evil, but he is adamant that he can differentiate between neurosis and a genuine case of possession.

According to Sarchie, the trouble with diagnosing a genuine case of possession is that demonic behaviour is virtually indistinguishable from many common mental and emotional disorders, so self-appointed exorcists must make their own on-the-spot psychological evaluations, which many are not qualified to do, or they must rely on 'secular psychiatrists' who don't believe in demons or the devil.

This leaves the burden of proof with the exorcist, and his only criteria for deciding if a case is genuine or not appear to be the subject's aversion to religious artefacts, fits of foul language and an understandable reluctance to be physically restrained and subjected to being sprayed with holy water and hours of intensive prayer. It's a highly subjective diagnosis of behaviour which mental health professionals would say is far more likely to have a psychological rather than a supernatural explanation, specifically a condition known as undifferentiated schizophrenia. The symptoms of this particularly distressing disorder could all too easily be 'mistaken' for those associated with possession by someone with no medical knowledge as it includes periods of lucidity and the ineffective nature of drugs which are normally effective against schizophrenia.

In one case he investigated, an 8-year-old girl displayed no signs of aggression, but spoke in fluent Latin which Sarchie says he found deeply distressing, yet 'speaking in tongues' is considered to be a miraculous phenomenon by many in the Church.

'THE DEVIL WON'T LET YOU GO'

When asked what advice he would give to would-be exorcists he answers bluntly that his advice is not to do it unless you can see people suffering and still want to help them. 'It's not something that you can do for a short time then move on as the Devil won't let you go and if he can't get you he'll get at you through a loved one.'

However, if someone is determined to fight the good fight they should pray for guidance to ensure that the impulse comes from God

'God never lets evil happen without something positive coming out of it'.

and not from personal ambition. It shouldn't be simply to witness phenomena or 'to see someone's head spin round'.

His parting advice reminds us of one of the reassurances which crime show presenters on TV impart to their viewers at the end of each show.

BIBLIOGRAPHY

Atwater, P.M.H., *Coming Back To Life* (Ballantine 1991)

Bradley, Mickey and Gordon, Dan, *Haunted Baseball: Ghosts, Curses, Legends, and Eerie Events* (The Lyons Press 2007)

Crookall, Robert, *The Supreme Adventure* (James Clarke & Co 1961)

Currie, Ian, *Visions Of Immortality* (Element 1998)

Danelek, Jeff, *The Case For Ghosts* (Llewellyn 2006)

Edward, John, *One Last Time* (Penguin Puttnam 2000)

Holroyd, S, *Mysteries Of The Inner Self* (Aldus 1978)

Moody, R.A., *The Light Beyond* (Rider 2005)

Moody, R.A., *Life After Life* (Mockingbird Books 1975)

Monroe, R.A., *Journeys Out Of The Body* (Doubleday 1971)

Morse, Melvin, *Closer To The Light* (Ivy Books 1991)

Muldoon, Sylvan, *The Phenomena Of Astral Projection* (Rider 1987)

Myers, F.W.H., *Human Personality And Its Survival Of Bodily Death* (Longmans, Green 1903)

Osis, K. and Haraldsson, E., *At The Hour Of Death* (Hastings House 1977)

Praagh, James Van, *Talking To Heaven* (Signet 1999)

Roland, Paul, *The Complete Book of Ghosts* (Arcturus 2006)

Roland, Paul, *Investigating The Unexplained* (Piatkus 2000)

Stall, Sam, *Suburban Legends: True Tales of Murder, Mayhem and Minivans* (Quirk Books 2006)

Wheeler, David R., *Journey To The Other Side* (Grosset & Dunlop 1976)

Wilson, Colin, *Afterlife* (Caxton Editions 1985)

Various Editors, *Mysteries of The Unknown* (Time Life 1987–91)

INTERNET RESOURCES

www.hauntedbaseball.com

www.ourcuriousworld.com (Jeff Danelek's site)

www.unexplainedstuff.com

www.legendsofamerica.com/LA-GhostlyLegends.html

www.theshadowlands.net

www.nderf.org

www.near-death.com

www.vanpraagh.com

www.johnedward.net

INDEX

PICTURE CREDITS